# pasta

# pasta

MURDOCH BOOKS

# Contents

# Short

# Penne all'arrabbiata

2 tablespoons olive oil
2 large garlic cloves, thinly sliced
1–2 medium-sized dried chillies
2 x 400 g (14 oz) tins tomatoes
400 g (14 oz) penne or rigatoni
1 basil sprig, torn into pieces

Heat the oil in a saucepan and add the garlic and chillies. Cook over low heat until the garlic is light golden brown. Turn the chillies over during cooking so both sides get a chance to infuse in the oil and turn slightly nutty in flavour. Add the tomatoes and season with salt. Cook gently, breaking up the tomatoes with a wooden spoon, for 20–30 minutes, or until the sauce is rich and thick.

Meanwhile, cook the pasta in a large saucepan of rapidly boiling salted water until al dente. Drain well and return to the pan to keep warm.

Add the basil to the sauce and season just before serving, tossed with the pasta. If you prefer a hotter sauce, break open the chilli to release the seeds.

Serves 4

# Tomato ditalini soup

2 tablespoons olive oil
1 large onion, finely chopped
2 celery stalks, finely chopped
3 vine-ripened tomatoes
1.5 litres (52 fl oz/6 cups) chicken
   or vegetable stock
90 g (3¼ oz/½ cup) ditalini

Heat the oil in a large saucepan over medium heat. Add the onion and celery and cook for 5 minutes, or until they have softened.

Score a cross in the base of each tomato, then place in a bowl of boiling water for 1 minute. Plunge the tomatoes into cold water and peel the skin away from the cross. Halve the tomatoes and scoop out the seeds with a teaspoon. Roughly chop the flesh.

Add the stock and tomato to the pan and bring to the boil. Add the pasta and cook for 10 minutes, or until al dente. Season and serve.

Serves 4

## Artichoke risoni

30 g (1 oz) butter
1 tablespoon olive oil
2 fennel bulbs, sliced
340 g (12 oz) marinated artichoke
  hearts, drained and chopped
300 ml (10½ fl oz) pouring
  (whipping) cream
1 tablespoon Dijon mustard
3 tablespoons dry white wine
50 g (1¾ oz/½ cup) grated parmesan
  cheese
375 g (13 oz) risoni
130 g (4¾ oz/2 cups) shredded
  English spinach leaves

Heat the butter and oil in a frying pan over medium heat, add the fennel and cook for 20 minutes, or until caramelised. Add the artichoke and cook for 5–10 minutes longer. Stir in the cream, mustard, white wine and grated parmesan and bring to the boil. Reduce the heat and simmer for 5 minutes.

Meanwhile, cook the pasta in a large saucepan of rapidly boiling salted water until al dente. Drain well and return to the pan to keep warm.

Add the risoni and spinach to the sauce and cook until the spinach has wilted. This is delicious served with toasted Italian bread.

Serves 4

# Pasta with baby spinach, pumpkin and tomato

750 g (1 lb 10 oz) sweet pumpkin (winter squash), such as butternut or jap
2 tablespoons parmesan-infused olive oil (see Notes)
16 garlic cloves, unpeeled
250 g (9 oz) cherry tomatoes, halved
500 g (1 lb 2 oz) orecchiette or penne
200 g (7 oz) baby spinach leaves
200 g (7 oz) marinated Persian feta cheese (see Notes)
3 tablespoons sherry vinegar
2 tablespoons walnut oil

Preheat the oven to 200°C (400°F/ Gas 6). Cut the pumpkin into large cubes, place in a roasting tin and drizzle with parmesan oil. Roast for 30 minutes, then add the garlic. Arrange the tomatoes on a baking tray. Place the vegetables in the oven and roast for 10–15 minutes, or until cooked. Don't overcook the tomatoes or they will turn to mush.

Meanwhile, cook the pasta in a large saucepan of rapidly boiling salted water until al dente. Drain well and return to the pan to keep warm.

Toss together the pasta, tomatoes, pumpkin, garlic and spinach in a large bowl. Drain the feta, reserving 3 tablespoons marinade. Whisk the reserved marinade, vinegar and walnut oil together. Pour over the pasta and sprinkle with pieces of the cheese.

Serves 4

Notes: Parmesan-infused olive oil is available at gourmet food stores and really adds depth of flavour. Persian feta is softer and creamier than other feta and is marinated in oil, herbs and garlic.

Variation: Toss in 200 g (7 oz) marinated Kalamata olives for added flavour.

# Bean soup with sausage

2 teaspoons olive oil
4 Italian sausages, diced
2 leeks, sliced
1 garlic clove, crushed
1 large carrot, finely diced
2 celery stalks, sliced
2 tablespoons plain (all-purpose) flour
2 beef stock (bouillon) cubes, crumbled
125 ml (4 fl oz/½ cup) dry white wine
125 g (4½ oz) small pasta shells
440 g (15½ oz) tinned mixed beans, drained and rinsed
1 teaspoon chopped chilli (optional)

Heat the oil in a large heavy-based saucepan and add the sausage. Cook over medium heat for 5 minutes or until golden, stirring regularly. Drain on paper towels.

Add the leek, garlic, carrot and celery to the pan and cook, stirring occasionally, for 2–3 minutes or until soft.

Add the flour and cook, stirring, for 1 minute. Add the stock cubes and wine and gradually stir in 2 litres (70 fl oz/8 cups) water. Bring to the boil, then reduce the heat and simmer for 10 minutes.

Add the pasta, beans and chilli (if using) to the pan. Increase the heat and cook for 8–10 minutes, or until the pasta is al dente. Return the sausage to the saucepan and season.

Serves 4–6

Variation: You can also use dried beans. Place in a bowl, cover with water and soak overnight. Drain, add to a large saucepan with water to come about 3 cm (1¼ inches) above the beans and simmer for 1 hour. Drain well before adding to the soup.

## Rotelle with chickpeas, tomato and parsley

375 g (13 oz) rotelle
1 tablespoon ground cumin
125 ml (4 fl oz/½ cup) olive oil
1 red onion, halved and thinly sliced
3 garlic cloves, crushed
400 g (14 oz) tinned chickpeas,
    drained
3 large tomatoes, diced
1 large handful chopped flat-leaf
    (Italian) parsley leaves
3 tablespoons lemon juice
grated parmesan cheese, for serving

Cook the pasta in a large saucepan of rapidly boiling salted water until al dente. Drain well and return to the pan to keep warm.

Meanwhile, heat a large frying pan over medium heat, add the cumin and cook, tossing, for 1 minute, or until fragrant. Remove from the pan. Heat half the oil in the same pan and cook the onion over medium heat for 2–3 minutes, or until soft. Stir in the garlic, chickpeas, tomato and parsley and stir until warmed through. Gently toss through the pasta.

Place the lemon juice, cumin and remaining oil in a jar with a lid and shake together well. Add the dressing to the saucepan with the pasta and chickpea mixture, return to low heat, stir until warmed through and season well. Serve hot with grated parmesan.

Serves 4

Variation: If serving cold, rinse the pasta under cold water before adding the chickpea mixture and do not return to the heat.

# Creamy pesto chicken penne

1 tablespoon olive oil
40 g (1½ oz) butter
400 g (14 oz) chicken breast fillets
170 g (6 oz) thin asparagus,
  cut into 4 cm (1½ inch) lengths
3 spring onions (scallions), chopped
4 garlic cloves, crushed
125 ml (4 fl oz/½ cup) pouring
  (whipping) cream
300 g (10½ oz) sour cream
185 ml (6 fl oz/¾ cup) chicken stock
100 g (3½ oz/1 cup) grated
  parmesan cheese
1 small handful basil leaves, finely
  chopped, plus whole leaves,
  for garnishing
2 tablespoons pine nuts, toasted
400 g (14 oz) penne

Heat the oil and half the butter in a large frying pan over high heat. Add the chicken and cook for 5 minutes on each side, or until just cooked. Remove, cover and cool, then cut into 1 cm (½ inch) slices.

Add the asparagus and spring onion to the pan, and cook for 2 minutes, or until the asparagus is just tender. Remove. Wipe out the pan with paper towels.

Reduce the heat to medium, add the remaining butter and the garlic, and cook for 2 minutes, or until pale gold. Add the cream, sour cream and stock, and simmer for 10 minutes, or until reduced slightly. Add the parmesan and basil, and stir for 2 minutes, or until the cheese has melted. Return the chicken and asparagus to the pan, add the pine nuts and cook for 2 minutes to heat through. Season.

Meanwhile, cook the pasta in a large saucepan of rapidly boiling salted water until al dente. Drain well. Combine the sauce and the pasta and garnish with basil leaves.

Serves 4

# Pasta with grilled capsicum

6 large red capsicum (peppers),
   halved
400 g (14 oz) pasta gnocchi (see Note)
2 tablespoons olive oil
1 onion, thinly sliced
3 garlic cloves, finely chopped
2 tablespoons shredded basil,
   plus whole leaves, for garnishing
shaved parmesan cheese,
   for garnishing

Cut the capsicum into large flattish pieces. Cook, skin side up, under a hot grill (broiler) until the skin blackens and blisters. Place in a plastic bag and leave to cool, then peel the skin.

Cook the pasta in a saucepan of rapidly boiling salted water until al dente. Drain well and return to the pan to keep warm

Meanwhile, heat the oil in a large frying pan, add the onion and garlic and cook over medium heat for 5 minutes, or until soft. Cut one capsicum into thin strips and add to the onion mixture.

Chop the remaining capsicum, then purée in a food processor until smooth. Add to the onion mixture and cook over low heat for 5 minutes, or until warmed through.

Toss the sauce through the hot pasta. Season, then stir in the shredded basil. Garnish with the basil leaves and parmesan.

Serves 4–6

Note: Not to be confused with the potato dumplings of the same name, pasta gnocchi is, as the name suggests, similar in shape to potato gnocchi. If unavailable, use small pasta shells or orecchiette.

## Penne with pumpkin, baked ricotta and prosciutto

500 g (1 lb 2 oz) penne
450 g (1 lb) butternut pumpkin (winter
  squash), cut into small cubes
3 tablespoons extra virgin olive oil
2 garlic cloves, crushed
100 g (3½ oz) semi-dried
  (sun-blushed) tomatoes, chopped
4 slices prosciutto, chopped
250 g (9 oz/1 cup) baked ricotta
  cheese, cut into small cubes
3 tablespoons shredded basil

Cook the pasta in a large saucepan of rapidly boiling salted water until al dente. Drain well and return to the pan to keep warm.

Meanwhile, cook the pumpkin in a saucepan of boiling water for 10–12 minutes, or until just tender, then drain.

Heat the oil in a large saucepan, add the garlic and cook over medium heat for 30 seconds. Add the tomato, prosciutto, pumpkin and penne and toss gently over low heat for 1–2 minutes, or until heated through.

Add the baked ricotta and the basil, season and serve immediately.

Serves 4

# Creamy rigatoni with chicken and tomato sauce

500 g (1 lb 2 oz) rigatoni
1 tablespoon olive oil
4 chicken breast fillets, thinly sliced
4 ripe tomatoes, diced
150 g (5½ oz/1 cup) sun-dried
  tomatoes in oil, thinly sliced
2 tablespoons sun-dried tomato paste
  (concentrated purée) (see Note)
1 handful small basil leaves
300 ml (10½ fl oz) pouring
  (whipping) cream
200 ml (7 fl oz) chicken stock

Cook the pasta in a large saucepan of rapidly boiling salted water until al dente. Drain well and return to the pan to keep warm.

Meanwhile, heat the oil in a deep frying pan and cook the chicken over high heat for 1–1½ minutes on each side, or until browned and cooked through. Remove from the pan and keep warm.

Return the frying pan to the heat and add the tomato, sun-dried tomato, tomato paste and half the basil leaves. Cook over medium heat for 5 minutes, or until the tomato starts to soften. Stir in the cream and chicken stock and bring to the boil, stirring constantly.

Reduce the heat and return the chicken to the pan. Add the warm rigatoni and season with pepper. Heat gently until the chicken and pasta are warmed through. Top with the remaining basil leaves and serve immediately.

Serves 4–6

Note: Sun-dried tomato paste is available in good supermarkets, or you can make your own by processing whole sun-dried tomatoes in oil with a little of their oil into a smooth paste.

## Pasta with clams

500 g (1 lb 2 oz) small shell pasta
1 tablespoon olive oil
2 garlic cloves, crushed
850 g (1 lb 14 oz) tinned chopped
  tomatoes
3 tablespoons dry red wine
2 tablespoons chopped flat-leaf
  (Italian) parsley
1 teaspoon white sugar
1 kg (2 lb 4 oz) clams (vongole) or
  pipis, soaked in cold water for
  30 minutes, then drained

Cook the pasta in a large saucepan of rapidly boiling salted water until al dente. Drain well and return to the pan to keep warm.

Meanwhile, heat the oil in a large saucepan. Add the garlic and cook over low heat for 30 seconds. Add the tomato, wine, parsley and sugar and season. Stir and bring to the boil. Reduce the heat and simmer, stirring occasionally, for 5 minutes.

Add the clams to the sauce and cook for 3–5 minutes, stirring occasionally, until opened. Discard any clams that do not open in the cooking time. Serve over the pasta.

Serves 4

## Penne with mushroom and herb sauce

2 tablespoons olive oil
500 g (1 lb 2 oz) button mushrooms,
   sliced
2 garlic cloves, crushed
2 teaspoons chopped marjoram
125 ml (4 fl oz/½ cup) dry white wine
80 ml (2½ fl oz/⅓ cup) pouring
   (whipping) cream
375 g (13 oz) penne
1 tablespoon lemon juice
1 teaspoon finely grated lemon zest
2 tablespoons chopped flat-leaf
   (Italian) parsley
50 g (1¾ oz/½ cup) grated parmesan
   cheese

Heat the oil in a large heavy-based frying pan over high heat. Add the mushrooms and cook for 3 minutes, stirring constantly to prevent the mushrooms from burning. Add the garlic and marjoram and cook for a further 2 minutes.

Add the white wine to the pan, reduce the heat and simmer for 5 minutes, or until nearly all the liquid has evaporated. Stir in the cream and cook over low heat for 5 minutes, or until the sauce has thickened.

Meanwhile, cook the penne in a large saucepan of rapidly boiling salted water until al dente. Drain well and return to the pan to keep warm.

Add the lemon juice, zest, parsley and half the parmesan to the sauce. Season and toss the penne through the sauce. Sprinkle with the remaining parmesan.

Serves 4

## Bacon and pea soup

4 slices bacon, diced (see Note)
50 g (1¾ oz) butter
1 large onion, finely chopped
1 celery stalk, chopped into small
    pieces
2 litres (70 fl oz/8 cups) chicken stock
150 g (5½ oz/1 cup) frozen peas
250 g (9 oz) risoni
2 tablespoons chopped flat-leaf
    (Italian) parsley

Put the bacon, butter, onion and celery in a large heavy-based saucepan. Cook for 5 minutes over low heat, stirring occasionally.

Add the stock and peas and simmer, covered, for 5 minutes. Increase the heat and add the pasta. Cook uncovered, stirring occasionally, for 5 minutes. Add the parsley and serve.

Serves 4–6

Note: Double-smoked bacon will give the best flavour for this recipe.

## Casarecci pasta with roasted tomatoes, rocket and goat's cheese

16 Roma (plum) tomatoes
1 small handful basil leaves, torn
400 g (14 oz) casarecci (see Note)
80 ml (2½ fl oz/⅓ cup) olive oil
2 garlic cloves, thinly sliced
2 tablespoons lemon juice
120 g (4¼ oz/4 cups) rocket (arugula), roughly chopped
2 tablespoons chopped flat-leaf (Italian) parsley
35 g (1¼ oz/⅓ cup) grated parmesan cheese
100 g (3½ oz) goat's cheese

Preheat the oven to 160°C (315°F/ Gas 2–3). Score a cross in the base of the tomatoes. Place in a heatproof bowl, and cover with boiling water. Leave for 30 seconds, then transfer to cold water and peel the skin away from the cross. Cut in half and place, cut side up, on a wire rack over a baking tray. Season and scatter with the basil leaves. Put the tray in the oven and bake for 3 hours.

Cook the pasta in a large saucepan of rapidly boiling salted water until al dente. Drain well and return to the pan to keep warm.

Heat the oil and garlic in a small saucepan over low–medium heat until it just begins to sizzle. Remove immediately and add to the pasta with the tomatoes, lemon juice, rocket, parsley and parmesan. Stir gently to combine, allowing the heat from the pasta to wilt the rocket. Serve topped with crumbled goat's cheese.

Serves 4

Note: Casarecci is a narrow, thin, rolled pasta. You can use fusilli too.

## Pasta with braised oxtail and celery

1.5 kg (3 lb 5 oz) oxtail, jointed
3 tablespoons plain (all-purpose) flour,
  seasoned (see Note)
3 tablespoons olive oil
1 onion, finely chopped
2 garlic cloves, crushed
500 ml (17 fl oz/2 cups) beef stock
425 g (15 oz) tin chopped tomatoes
250 ml (9 fl oz/1 cup) dry white wine
6 whole cloves
2 bay leaves
3 celery stalks, finely chopped
500 g (1 lb 2 oz) penne
30 g (1 oz) butter
3 tablespoons grated parmesan
  cheese

Preheat the oven to 160°C (315°F/ Gas 2–3). Dust the oxtail in the seasoned flour, shaking off any excess. Heat half the oil in a large frying pan and brown the oxtail over high heat in batches. Transfer the meat to a large ovenproof dish.

Wipe the frying pan clean with paper towels, add the remaining oil and the onion and garlic. Cook over low heat until the onion is tender. Stir in the stock, tomato, wine, cloves and bay leaves and season. Bring to the boil and then pour over the oxtail.

Bake, covered, for 2½–3 hours. Add the celery and bake, uncovered, for another 30 minutes.

Meanwhile, cook the pasta in a large saucepan of rapidly boiling salted water until al dente. Drain well and return to the pan to keep warm. Toss with the butter and parmesan. Serve the oxtail and sauce with the pasta.

Serves 4

Note: Add seasonings of your choice, such as herbs, salt, pepper or dried mustard to plain flour.

## Penne with bacon, ricotta and basil sauce

2 teaspoons olive oil
2 slices bacon, chopped
2–3 garlic cloves, crushed
1 onion, finely chopped
2 spring onions (scallions),
  finely chopped
250 g (9 oz/1 cup) ricotta cheese
1 handful basil leaves, finely chopped,
  plus whole leaves, for garnishing
325 g (11½ oz) penne
8 cherry tomatoes, halved

Heat the oil in a saucepan, add the bacon, garlic, onion and spring onion and stir over medium heat for 5 minutes, or until cooked. Remove from the heat, stir in the ricotta and chopped basil and beat until smooth.

Cook the pasta in a large saucepan of rapidly boiling salted water until al dente. Just prior to draining the pasta, add about 250 ml (9 fl oz/1 cup) of the pasta cooking water to the ricotta mixture to thin the sauce. Add more water if you prefer an even thinner sauce and season.

Drain the pasta and stir the sauce and tomato halves through the pasta. Garnish with small fresh basil leaves.

*Serves 4*

## Macaroni cheese with pancetta

390 g (13¾ oz/2½ cups) macaroni
75 g (2½ oz) pancetta, diced
500 ml (17 fl oz/2 cups) pouring
   (whipping) cream
125 g (4½ oz/1 cup) grated
   cheddar cheese
260 g (9¼ oz/2 cups) grated
   Gruyère cheese
100 g (3½ oz/1 cup) grated
   parmesan cheese
1 garlic clove, crushed
2 teaspoons Dijon mustard
½ teaspoon paprika
2 tablespoons snipped chives,
   plus extra for garnishing

Cook the pasta in a large saucepan of rapidly boiling salted water until al dente. Drain well and return to the pan to keep warm.

Meanwhile, place the pancetta in a large saucepan and cook over high heat, stirring, for 4 minutes, or until well browned and slightly crisp. Drain on paper towels. Reduce the heat to medium, stir in the cream and simmer. Add the cheeses, garlic, mustard and paprika and stir for 5 minutes, or until the cheeses have melted and the sauce has thickened. Season.

Add the macaroni and pancetta and stir for 1 minute, or until heated through. Stir in the chives, garnish with the extra chives and serve.

Serves 4

## Pasta with pork and fennel sausages

6 Italian pork and fennel sausages
  (about 550 g/1 lb 4 oz)
1 tablespoon olive oil
1 small red onion, finely chopped
2–3 garlic cloves, crushed
½ teaspoon chilli flakes
300 g (10½ oz) field or button
  mushrooms, thinly sliced
2 x 400 g (14 oz) tins diced tomatoes
1 tablespoon finely chopped thyme
500 g (1 lb 2 oz) penne
grated parmesan cheese, for serving

Heat the oil in a large saucepan over medium–high heat and cook the onion for 3–4 minutes, or until fragrant and transparent. Add the garlic, chilli flakes, mushrooms and crumbled sausage meat. Cook over high heat, stirring gently to mash the sausage meat, for 4–5 minutes, or until the meat is evenly browned. If necessary, use a tablespoon to remove any excess fat from the pan, leaving about a tablespoon of oil. Continue to cook, stirring once or twice, for 10 minutes.

Stir in the tomato and thyme, then bring the sauce to the boil. Cover and cook over medium–low heat for 20 minutes, stirring occasionally to make sure the sauce doesn't stick to the bottom of the pan.

Meanwhile, cook the pasta in a large saucepan of rapidly boiling salted water until al dente. Drain well, then add to the sauce, stirring to combine. Garnish with parmesan.

Serves 4

# Hearty Italian bean and pasta soup

1 tablespoon olive oil
1 onion, finely chopped
3 garlic cloves, crushed
600 g (1 lb 5 oz) tinned mixed beans, drained and rinsed
1.75 litres (61 fl oz/7 cups) chicken stock (see Note)
100 g (3½ oz) small pasta shells
1 tablespoon chopped tarragon

Heat the oil in a saucepan over low heat. Add the onion and cook for 5 minutes, then add the garlic and cook for a further 1 minute, stirring frequently. Add the beans and chicken stock and then cover the pan with a lid.

Increase the heat and bring to the boil. Add the pasta and cook until al dente. Stir in the tarragon and season.

Serves 4

Note: The flavour of this soup is really enhanced by using a good-quality stock. Either make your own or use the cartons of liquid stock that are available at the supermarket.

## Chicken and eggplant pasta

375 g (13 oz) penne
100 ml (3½ fl oz) olive oil
4 slender eggplants (aubergines),
  thinly sliced on the diagonal
2 chicken breast fillets
2 teaspoons lemon juice
1 large handful flat-leaf (Italian) parsley
  leaves, chopped
270 g (9½ oz) chargrilled red
  capsicum (pepper), drained
  and sliced (see Note)
150 g (5½ oz) fresh asparagus,
  trimmed, blanched and cut into
  short lengths
90 g (3¼ oz) semi-dried (sun-blushed)
  tomatoes, thinly sliced

Cook the pasta in a large saucepan of rapidly boiling salted water until al dente. Drain well and return to the pan to keep warm.

Meanwhile, heat 2 tablespoons of the oil in a large frying pan over high heat and cook the eggplant for 4–5 minutes, or until golden and cooked through.

Heat a lightly oiled chargrill pan over high heat and cook the chicken for 5 minutes each side, or until browned and cooked through. Thickly slice.

Combine the lemon juice, parsley and remaining oil in a small screw-top jar and shake well.

Return the pasta to the heat, toss through the dressing, chicken, eggplant, capsicum, asparagus and tomato until well mixed and warmed through. Season and serve.

Serves 4

Note: You can buy jars of chargrilled capsicum at the supermarket; otherwise, visit your local deli.

## Salmon and pasta mornay

400 g (14 oz) small shell pasta
30 g (1 oz) butter
6 spring onions (scallions), chopped
2 garlic cloves, crushed
1 tablespoon plain (all-purpose) flour
250 ml (9 fl oz/1 cup) milk
250 g (9 oz/1 cup) sour cream
1 tablespoon lemon juice
425 g (15 oz) tinned salmon,
   drained and flaked
1 handful flat-leaf (Italian) parsley
   leaves, chopped

Cook the pasta in a large saucepan of rapidly boiling salted water until al dente. Drain well and return to the pan to keep warm.

Meanwhile, melt the butter in a saucepan and cook the spring onion and garlic over low heat for 3 minutes or until soft. Add the flour and stir for 1 minute. Mix together the milk, sour cream and lemon juice and slowly add to the pan, stirring constantly. Stir over medium heat for 3 minutes or until the sauce boils and thickens.

Add the salmon and parsley to the sauce and stir for 1 minute to heat through. Toss with the pasta and season before serving.

Serves 4

Variation: Use tinned tuna instead of salmon. Add 1 teaspoon of mustard to the sauce.

## Orecchiette with broccoli

750 g (1 lb 10 oz) broccoli,
    cut into florets
450 g (1 lb) orecchiette
3 tablespoons extra virgin olive oil
½ teaspoon chilli flakes
30 g (1 oz/⅓ cup) grated pecorino
    or parmesan cheese

Blanch the broccoli in a saucepan of boiling salted water for 5 minutes, or until just tender. Remove with a slotted spoon, drain well and return the water to the boil. Cook the pasta in the boiling water until al dente, then drain well and return to the pan.

Meanwhile, heat the oil in a heavy-based frying pan and add the chilli flakes and broccoli. Increase the heat to medium and cook, stirring, for 5 minutes, or until the broccoli is well coated and beginning to break apart. Season. Add to the pasta, toss in the cheese and serve.

Serves 6

# Pasta Amatriciana

6 thin slices pancetta
 or 3 slices bacon
1 kg (2 lb 4 oz) very ripe tomatoes
500 g (1 lb 2 oz) pasta (see Notes)
1 tablespoon olive oil
1 small onion, finely chopped
2 teaspoons finely chopped chilli

Finely chop the pancetta. Score a cross in the base of each tomato. Soak in boiling water for 1 minute, then drain and plunge into cold water briefly. Peel the skin away from the cross. Halve the tomatoes, remove the seeds and chop the flesh.

Cook the pasta in a large saucepan of rapidly boiling salted water until al dente. Drain well and return to the pan to keep warm.

Meanwhile, heat the oil in a heavy-based frying pan. Add the pancetta, onion and chilli and stir over medium heat for 3 minutes. Add the tomato and season. Reduce the heat and simmer for 3 minutes. Add the sauce to the pasta and toss until well combined.

Serves 4–6

Notes: It is believed this dish originated in the Italian town of Amatrice, where bacon is a prized local product. For a change from ordinary tomatoes, try Roma (plum) tomatoes, which have a rich flavour when cooked. Traditionally, bucatini is served with this sauce, but you can use any pasta you prefer.

## Spinach and ricotta gnocchi

4 slices white bread
125 ml (4 fl oz/½ cup) milk
500 g (1 lb 2 oz) frozen spinach,
   thawed and squeezed
250 g (9 oz/1 cup) ricotta cheese
2 eggs
60 g (2¼ oz) grated parmesan cheese
3 tablespoons plain (all-purpose) flour
shaved parmesan cheese, for serving

*Garlic butter sauce*
100 g (3½ oz) butter
2 garlic cloves, crushed
1 ripe tomato, diced
3 tablespoons chopped basil

Remove the crusts from the bread and discard. Soak the bread in milk in a shallow dish for 10 minutes. Squeeze out any excess milk from the bread. Place the bread, spinach, ricotta, eggs and parmesan in a bowl and mix thoroughly. Refrigerate, covered, for 1 hour. Fold the flour in well.

Lightly dust your hands in flour and roll heaped teaspoons of the bread mixture into dumplings. Lower batches of the gnocchi into a large saucepan of boiling salted water. Cook each batch for about 2 minutes, or until the gnocchi rise to the surface. Transfer to a serving plate and keep warm.

To make the sauce, combine all the ingredients in a small saucepan and cook over medium heat for 3 minutes, or until the butter is nutty brown. Drizzle over the gnocchi and scatter with the parmesan.

Serves 4–6

## Chicken and vegetable soup

1 tablespoon olive oil
1 carrot, sliced
1 leek, chopped
2 chicken thigh fillets, cut into
  bite-sized pieces
3 tablespoons ditalini
  or other small pasta
1 litre (35 fl oz/4 cups) vegetable stock
2 ripe tomatoes, diced
crusty bread, to serve

Heat the oil in a saucepan and cook the carrot and leek over medium heat for 4 minutes, or until soft. Add the chicken and cook for a further 2 minutes, or until the chicken has changed colour.

Add the pasta and the vegetable stock, cover and bring to the boil. Reduce the heat and simmer for 10 minutes, or until the pasta is cooked. Add the tomato halfway through the cooking. Season and serve with crusty bread.

Serves 4

# Zucchini pasta bake

200 g (7 oz) risoni
40 g (1½ oz) butter
4 spring onions (scallions), thinly sliced
400 g (14 oz) zucchini (courgettes),
    grated
4 eggs
125 ml (4 fl oz/½ cup) pouring
    (whipping) cream
100 g (3½ oz) ricotta cheese
    (see Note)
100 g (3½ oz/⅔ cup) grated
    mozzarella cheese
75 g (2½ oz/¾ cup) grated
    parmesan cheese

Preheat the oven to 180°C (350°F/
Gas 4). Cook the pasta in a large
saucepan of rapidly boiling water until
al dente. Drain well.

Meanwhile, heat the butter in a frying
pan, add the spring onion and cook
for 1 minute, then add the zucchini
and cook for a further 4 minutes, or
until soft. Cool slightly.

Combine the eggs, cream, ricotta,
mozzarella, risoni and half of the
parmesan, then stir in the zucchini
mixture. Season well. Spoon into
four 500 ml (17 fl oz/2 cup) greased
ovenproof dishes, but not to the brim.
Sprinkle with the remaining parmesan
and cook for 25–30 minutes, or until
firm and golden.

Serves 4

Note: With such simple flavours, it is
important to use good-quality fresh
ricotta from a delicatessen or the deli
section of your local supermarket.

## Crab, Camembert and fusilli frittata

90 g (3¼ oz/1 cup) fusilli
1 tablespoon olive oil
1 very small red onion, finely chopped
1 large Roma (plum) tomato,
    roughly chopped
60 g (2¼ oz) semi-dried (sun-blushed)
    tomatoes, roughly chopped
2 tablespoons finely chopped
    coriander (cilantro) leaves
150 g (5½ oz/⅔ cup) cooked fresh
    or tinned crabmeat
150 g (5½ oz) Camembert cheese,
    rind removed, cut into small pieces
6 eggs, plus 2 egg yolks

Cook the pasta in a large saucepan of rapidly boiling salted water until al dente. Drain well and set aside to cool a little.

Meanwhile, heat half the oil in a small frying pan over low heat, add the onion and cook for 4–5 minutes, or until softened but not browned. Transfer to a bowl and add the Roma tomato, semi-dried tomato and coriander. Squeeze out any excess moisture from the crabmeat and add to the bowl. Add half the cheese and the cooled pasta. Mix well. Beat together the eggs and yolks, then stir into the frittata mixture. Season.

Heat the remaining oil in the frying pan, pour in the frittata mixture and cook over low heat for 25 minutes. Preheat the grill (broiler) to low. Scatter the remaining Camembert over the frittata before placing it under the grill for 10–15 minutes, or until cooked and golden brown on top. Remove from the grill and leave for 5 minutes. Cut into slices to serve.

Serves 4–6

## Pasta with ricotta, chilli and herbs

500 g (1 lb 2 oz) penne
3 tablespoons olive oil
3 garlic cloves, crushed
2 teaspoons finely chopped chilli
2 large handfuls flat-leaf (Italian)
    parsley leaves, roughly chopped
1 handful basil leaves, shredded
2 large handfuls oregano leaves,
    roughly chopped
200 g (7 oz) ricotta cheese, cut into
    small cubes

Cook the pasta in a large saucepan of rapidly boiling salted water until al dente. Drain well and return to the pan to keep warm.

Meanwhile, heat the oil in a non-stick heavy-based frying pan. Add the garlic and chilli to the pan and stir for 1 minute over low heat. Pour over the pasta and add the parsley, basil and oregano. Season and toss well. Add the ricotta and serve immediately.

Serves 4

## Country pumpkin and pasta soup

750 g (1 lb 10 oz) pumpkin
(winter squash) (see Note)
2 all-purpose potatoes
1 tablespoon olive oil
30 g (1 oz) butter
1 large onion, finely chopped
2 garlic cloves, crushed
3 litres (105 fl oz/12 cups) chicken
stock
125 g (4½ oz) soup pasta
1 tablespoon chopped flat-leaf (Italian)
parsley, for serving

Peel the pumpkin and potatoes and chop into small cubes. Heat the oil and butter in a large saucepan. Add the onion and garlic and cook, stirring, for 5 minutes over low heat.

Add the pumpkin, potato and chicken stock. Increase the heat, cover and cook for 8 minutes, or until the vegetables are tender.

Add the pasta and cook, stirring occasionally, for 5 minutes or until the pasta is al dente. Serve immediately, sprinkled with the parsley.

Serves 4–6

Note: Butternut or jap pumpkin will give this soup the sweetest flavour.

## Risoni risotto with mushrooms and pancetta

1 tablespoon butter
2 garlic cloves, finely chopped
150 g (5½ oz) piece pancetta, diced
400 g (14 oz) button mushrooms, sliced
500 g (1 lb 2 oz) risoni
1 litre (35 fl oz/ 4 cups) chicken stock
125 ml (4 fl oz/½ cup) pouring (whipping) cream
50 g (1¾ oz/½ cup) grated parmesan cheese
1 large handful flat-leaf (Italian) parsley leaves, finely chopped

Heat the butter in a saucepan, add the garlic and cook over medium heat for 30 seconds. Increase the heat to high, add the pancetta and cook for a further 3–5 minutes, or until crisp. Add the mushrooms and cook for 3–5 minutes, or until softened.

Add the risoni, stir until it is coated in the mixture, then add the stock and bring to the boil. Reduce the heat to medium and cook, covered, for 15–20 minutes, or until nearly all the liquid has evaporated and the risoni is tender.

Stir in the cream and cook, uncovered, for 3 minutes, stirring occasionally until the cream is absorbed. Stir in nearly all of the parmesan and parsley and season. Divide among serving bowls and serve with remaining parmesan.

Serves 4–6

# Penne with rosemary and prosciutto

1 tablespoon olive oil
6 thin slices prosciutto, chopped
1 onion, finely chopped
820 g (1 lb 13 oz) tinned chopped
tomatoes
1 tablespoon chopped rosemary
(see Note)
500 g (1 lb 2 oz) penne or macaroni
50 g (1¾ oz/½ cup) grated parmesan
cheese, for serving

Heat the oil in a heavy-based frying pan. Add the prosciutto and onion and cook, stirring occasionally, over low heat for 5 minutes or until the prosciutto is golden and the onion has softened.

Add the tomatoes and rosemary to the pan, season and simmer for 10 minutes.

Meanwhile, cook the pasta in a large saucepan of rapidly boiling salted water until al dente. Drain well. Divide among warmed serving bowls and top with the sauce. Sprinkle with parmesan and serve immediately.

Serves 4–6

Note: Rosemary, commonly used in Mediterranean cookery, adds a distinctive flavour to this dish.

# Eggplant, ricotta and pasta pots

200 g (7 oz) straight macaroni
125 ml (4 fl oz/½ cup) light olive oil
1 large eggplant (aubergine), cut
  lengthways into 1 cm (½ inch) slices
1 small onion, finely chopped
2 garlic cloves, crushed
400 g (14 oz) tinned diced tomatoes
400 g (14 oz) ricotta cheese
100 g (3½ oz/1 cup) coarsely grated
  parmesan cheese
1 handful basil leaves, shredded,
  plus extra for garnishing

Preheat the oven to 180°C (350°F/ Gas 4). Cook the macaroni in a large saucepan of salted boiling water until al dente. Drain.

Heat 2 tablespoons of oil in a non-stick frying pan over medium heat. Cook the eggplant in three batches for 2–3 minutes each side, or until golden, adding 2 tablespoons of oil with each batch. Remove and drain well on crumpled paper towels. Add the onion and garlic to the frying pan and cook over medium heat for 2–3 minutes, or until just golden. Add the tomato and cook for 5 minutes, or until the sauce is pulpy and most of the liquid has evaporated. Season, then remove from the heat.

Combine the ricotta, parmesan and shredded basil in a large bowl, then mix in the pasta. Line the base and sides of four 375 ml (13 fl oz/1½ cup) ramekins with eggplant, trimming any overhanging pieces. Top with half the pasta mix, pressing down firmly. Spoon on the tomato sauce, then cover with the remaining pasta mixture. Bake for 10–15 minutes, or until heated through and golden on top. Stand for 5 minutes, then run a knife around the ramekin to loosen. Invert onto plates and garnish with basil leaves.

Serves 4

## Pasta with pumpkin and feta

1 kg (2 lb 4 oz) butternut pumpkin
  (winter squash), peeled and cut
  into 2 cm (³/₄ inch) chunks
1 red onion, thinly sliced
8 garlic cloves, unpeeled
1 tablespoon rosemary leaves
80 ml (2½ fl oz/¹/₃ cup) olive oil
400 g (14 oz) short pasta
200 g (7 oz) marinated feta cheese,
  crumbled
2 tablespoons grated parmesan
  cheese
2 tablespoons finely chopped flat-leaf
  (Italian) parsley

Preheat the oven to 200°C (400°F/ Gas 6). Put the pumpkin, onion, garlic and rosemary in a roasting tin, then drizzle with 1 tablespoon of the oil. Season. Using your hands, rub the oil over all the ingredients until well coated. Roast for 30 minutes, or until the pumpkin is soft and starting to caramelise.

Cook the pasta in a saucepan of boiling salted water until al dente.

Squeeze the roasted garlic out of its skin and place it in a bowl with the remaining oil. Mash with a fork.

Add the garlic oil to the hot pasta, then the remaining ingredients. Toss well and season.

Serves 4

# Potato gnocchi with tomato and basil sauce

1 kg (2 lb 4 oz) all-purpose potatoes,
  roughly chopped
30 g (1 oz) butter
250 g (9 oz/1¾ cups) plain
  (all-purpose) flour
2 eggs, lightly beaten
grated parmesan cheese, for serving

*Tomato sauce*
1 tablespoon oil
1 onion, chopped
1 celery stalk, chopped
2 carrots, chopped
850 g (1 lb 14 oz) tinned chopped
  tomatoes
1 teaspoon white sugar
1 very large handful basil, chopped

To make the tomato sauce, heat the oil in a large frying pan and cook the onion, celery and carrots for 5 minutes, stirring regularly. Add the tomato and sugar and season. Bring to the boil, reduce the heat to very low and simmer for 20 minutes. Mix until smooth in a food processor. Add the basil leaves and set aside.

To make the gnocchi, cook the potatoes in boiling water for 15 minutes or until very tender. Drain well and mash until smooth. Using a wooden spoon, stir in the butter and the flour, then mix in the eggs. Leave to cool.

Turn the potato mixture out onto a floured surface and divide in two. Roll each half into a long sausage shape. Cut into 3–4 cm (1¼–1½ inch) pieces and press each piece with the back of a fork to give the gnocchi ridges.

Bring a large saucepan of salted water to the boil, add the gnocchi and cook for 3 minutes, or until they rise to the surface. Drain with a slotted spoon and serve with the tomato sauce and grated parmesan cheese.

Serves 4–6

## Penne with rustic lentil sauce

1 litre (35 fl oz/4 cups) vegetable
  or chicken stock
350 g (12 oz) penne
80 ml (2½ fl oz/⅓ cup) virgin olive oil,
  plus extra for serving
1 onion, chopped
2 carrots, diced
3 celery stalks, diced
3 garlic cloves, crushed
1¼ tablespoon chopped thyme
400 g (14 oz) tinned lentils, drained

Boil the chicken stock in a large saucepan for 10 minutes, or until reduced by half. Meanwhile, cook the pasta in a large saucepan of rapidly boiling salted water until al dente. Drain well and toss with 2 tablespoons of the olive oil.

Heat the remaining oil in a large, deep frying pan, add the onion, carrot and celery and cook over medium heat for 10 minutes, or until browned. Add two-thirds of the crushed garlic and 1 tablespoon of the thyme and cook for a further 1 minute. Add the stock, bring to the boil and cook for 8 minutes, or until tender. Stir in the lentils and heat through.

Stir in the remaining garlic and thyme and season well—the stock should be slightly syrupy at this point. Combine the pasta with the lentil sauce in a large bowl and drizzle with olive oil to serve.

Serves 4

## Roasted sweet potato and ditalini patties

800 g (1 lb 12 oz) orange sweet
  potatoes
90 g (3¼ oz/½ cup) ditalini
30 g (1 oz) pine nuts, toasted
2 garlic cloves, crushed
1 small handful basil leaves,
  finely chopped
60 g (2¼ oz) grated parmesan cheese
35 g (1¼ oz/⅓ cup) dry breadcrumbs
plain (all-purpose) flour, for dusting
olive oil, for shallow-frying

Preheat the oven to 250°C (500°F/ Gas 9). Pierce the whole sweet potatoes several times with a fork, place in a roasting tin and roast for about 1 hour, or until soft. Cool.

Meanwhile, cook the pasta in a large saucepan of rapidly boiling salted water until al dente. Drain well and rinse under cold water.

Peel the sweet potato and mash. Add the pine nuts, garlic, basil, parmesan, breadcrumbs and pasta and mix together. Season.

Shape the mixture into eight even patties with floured hands, then lightly dust the patties with flour. Heat the oil in a large frying pan and cook the patties in batches over medium heat for 2 minutes each side, or until golden and heated through. Drain on crumpled paper towels, sprinkle with salt and serve immediately.

Serves 4

Note: If you don't have much time, drop spoonfuls of the mixture into the pan and flatten with an oiled spatula.

Serving suggestion: The patties are great with aïoli—mix 1 clove of crushed garlic into 90 g (3¼ oz/ ⅓ cup) mayonnaise with a squeeze of lemon juice and season well.

## Orecchiette with cauliflower, bacon and pecorino

750 g (1 lb 10 oz) cauliflower,
  cut into florets
500 g (1 lb 2 oz) orecchiette
  (see Note)
125 ml (4 fl oz/1/2 cup) olive oil,
  plus extra, to drizzle
150 g (51/2 oz) bacon, diced
2 garlic cloves, finely chopped
80 g (23/4 oz/1/2 cup) pine nuts, toasted
45 g (11/2 oz/1/2 cup) grated
  pecorino cheese
1 small handful flat-leaf (Italian) parsley
  leaves, chopped
60 g (21/4 oz/3/4 cup) fresh
  breadcrumbs, toasted

Bring a large saucepan of boiling salted water to the boil and cook the cauliflower for 5–6 minutes, or until tender. Drain.

Cook the pasta in a large saucepan of boiling salted water until al dente.

Heat the oil in a frying pan and cook the bacon over medium heat for 4–5 minutes, or until just crisp. Add the garlic and cook for 1 minute, or until just beginning to turn golden. Add the cauliflower and toss well.

Add the cooked pasta to the pan with the pine nuts, pecorino, parsley and two-thirds of the breadcrumbs and mix. Season, sprinkle with the remaining breadcrumbs and drizzle with a little extra oil.

Serves 4

Note: Orecchiette means 'little ears' in Italian, and the name of the pasta is a literal description of the shape— although some brands look more like curls than ears. If unavailable, use small pasta shells.

## Pasta with tomato and basil sauce

500 g (1 lb 2 oz) penne
80 ml (2½ fl oz/⅓ cup) extra virgin
    olive oil
4 garlic cloves, crushed
4 anchovies, finely chopped
2 small red chillies, seeded
    and finely chopped
6 large vine-ripened tomatoes,
    peeled, seeded and diced
80 ml (2½ fl oz/⅓ cup) white wine
1 tablespoon tomato paste
    (concentrated purée)
2 teaspoons white sugar
2 tablespoons finely chopped flat-leaf
    (Italian) parsley
3 tablespoons shredded basil

Cook the pasta in a large saucepan of rapidly boiling salted water until al dente. Drain well and return to the pan to keep warm.

Meanwhile, heat the oil in a frying pan and cook the garlic for 30 seconds. Stir in the anchovy and chilli and cook for a further 30 seconds. Add the tomato and cook for 2 minutes over high heat. Add the wine, tomato paste and sugar and simmer, covered, for 10 minutes, or until thickened.

Toss the tomato sauce through the pasta with the herbs and season.

Serves 4

## Penne with bacon, sun-dried tomatoes and lemon

250 g (9 oz) penne
3 tablespoons olive oil
3 slices bacon, chopped
1 onion, chopped
80 ml (2½ fl oz/⅓ cup) lemon juice
1 tablespoon thyme leaves
50 g (1¾ oz/⅓ cup) chopped
  sun-dried tomatoes
80 g (2¾ oz/½ cup) pine nuts,
  toasted

Cook the pasta in a large saucepan of rapidly boiling salted water until al dente. Drain well and return to the pan to keep warm.

Heat the oil in a large saucepan. Add the bacon and onion and stir over medium heat for 4 minutes or until the bacon is brown and the onion has softened. Add the pasta, lemon juice, thyme, tomato and pine nuts. Stir over low heat for 2 minutes to heat through. Serve immediately.

Serves 4

Hint: Sun-dried tomatoes will become bitter if heated too much.

Variation: Use pancetta instead of bacon, if preferred.

## Creamy pasta with peas and prosciutto

100 g (3½ oz) prosciutto, thinly sliced
3 teaspoons oil
2 eggs
250 ml (9 fl oz/1 cup) pouring
  (whipping) cream
35 g (1¼ oz/⅓ cup) grated
  parmesan cheese
2 tablespoons chopped flat-leaf
  (Italian) parsley
1 tablespoon snipped chives
250 g (9 oz) fresh or frozen peas
500 g (1 lb 2 oz) small pasta shells
  or gnocchi

Cut the prosciutto into thin strips. Heat the oil in a frying pan over medium heat, add the prosciutto and cook for 2 minutes, or until crisp. Drain on paper towels. Whisk together the eggs, cream, parmesan and herbs in a large bowl.

Bring a large saucepan of salted water to the boil. Add the peas and cook for 5 minutes, or until just tender. Leaving the pan on the heat, use a slotted spoon and transfer the peas to the bowl of cream mixture, and then add 3 tablespoons of the cooking liquid to the same bowl. Using a potato masher or the back of a fork, roughly mash the peas.

Add the pasta to the boiling water and cook until al dente. Drain well, then return to the pan. Add the cream mixture, then warm through over low heat, gently stirring for about 30 seconds until the pasta is coated in the sauce. Season and divide among warmed plates, top with the prosciutto and serve immediately.

Serves 4

Note: Be careful not to overheat or cook for too long or the egg will begin to scramble.

## Orecchiette with mushrooms, pancetta and smoked mozzarella

400 g (14 oz) orecchiette
2 tablespoons olive oil
150 g (5½ oz) pancetta, cut into
   thin strips
200 g (7 oz) button mushrooms, sliced
2 leeks, sliced
250 ml (9 fl oz/1 cup) pouring
   (whipping) cream
200 g (7 oz) smoked mozzarella,
   cut into 1 cm (½ inch) cubes
8 basil leaves, roughly torn

Cook the orecchiette in a large saucepan of rapidly boiling salted water until al dente. Drain well and return to the pan to keep warm.

Meanwhile, heat the oil in a large frying pan and sauté the pancetta, mushrooms and leek over medium–high heat for 5 minutes. Stir in the cream and season with pepper—the pancetta should provide enough salty flavour. Simmer over low heat for 5 minutes, or until the pasta is ready. Drain the pasta and stir into the frying pan. Add the mozzarella and basil and toss lightly.

Serves 4

Note: To make this healthier, you can use half chicken stock and half cream instead of all cream. Smoked provolone can be used instead of the mozzarella, if preferred.

## Roasted tomato and pasta salad with pesto

140 ml (4½ fl oz) olive oil
500 g (1 lb 2 oz) cherry tomatoes
5 garlic cloves, unpeeled
400 g (14 oz) penne
90 g (3¼ oz/⅓ cup) pesto
3 tablespoons balsamic vinegar
basil leaves, for garnishing

Preheat the oven to 180°C (350°F/ Gas 4). Place 2 tablespoons of oil in a roasting dish and place in the hot oven for 5 minutes. Add the tomatoes and garlic to the dish, season well and toss until the tomatoes are well coated. Return to the oven and roast for 30 minutes.

Meanwhile, cook the pasta in a large saucepan of rapidly boiling water until al dente. Drain and transfer to a large serving bowl.

Squeeze the flesh from the roasted garlic cloves into a bowl. Add the remaining olive oil, the pesto, vinegar and 3 tablespoons of the tomato cooking juices. Season and toss to combine. Add to the pasta and mix well, ensuring that the pasta is coated in the dressing. Gently stir in the cherry tomatoes, then scatter with basil. This salad can be prepared up to 4 hours ahead, and served warm or cold.

Serves 4

# Farfalle with tuna, capers and lemon cream sauce

500 g (1 lb 2 oz) tuna fillet, trimmed
400 g (14 oz) farfalle pasta
300 ml (10 fl oz) cream
large handful baby rocket (arugula)
3 teaspoons small capers, drained
1½ teaspoons finely grated lemon rind
60 ml (2 fl oz/¼ cup) teaspoons
  lemon juice
pinch dried chilli flakes (optional)

Using a large, sharp knife, cut the tuna into 1 cm (½ inch) pieces and set aside.

Cook the pasta in boiling, salted water for 13 minutes or according to packet instructions until al dente. Drain well.

Meanwhile, combine the cream, rocket and capers in a small saucepan or frying pan over a medium–low heat, cover and bring to a gentle boil. Add the lemon rind and stir to combine well, then cook for 1 minute or until the rocket is just wilted. Add the tuna, lemon juice and pasta to the pan, toss to combine well and heat for about 1 minute to warm the tuna through. Season to taste with sea salt, freshly ground black pepper and chilli flakes, if using. Serve immediately.

Serves 4

## Penne with tomato and onion jam and olives

3 tablespoons olive oil
4 red onions, sliced
1 tablespoon soft brown sugar
2 tablespoons balsamic vinegar
2 x 400 g (14 oz) tins chopped
   tomatoes
500 g (1 lb 2 oz) penne
150 g (5½ oz) small pitted black olives
   or pitted and halved Kalamata olives
75 g (2½ oz/¾ cup) shredded
   parmesan cheese

Heat the oil in a non-stick frying pan over medium heat. Add the onion and sugar and cook for 25–30 minutes, or until caramelised.

Stir in the vinegar, bring to the boil and cook for 5 minutes. Add the tomatoes, return to the boil, then reduce the heat to medium–low and simmer for 25 minutes, or until the tomatoes are reduced and jam-like.

Cook the pasta in a large saucepan of rapidly boiling salted water until al dente. Drain, then return to the pan. Add the tomato mixture and olives and stir to combine well. Season and garnish with the grated parmesan.

Serves 4

Notes: Caramelised onions will keep for a few days, if covered with oil and stored in the refrigerator. The onions can be combined with goat's cheese to make a quick puff pastry tart or used as a pizza topping.

## Porcini mushroom and walnut penne

20 g (¾ oz) dried porcini mushrooms
400 g (14 oz) penne
2 tablespoons olive oil
1 onion, finely chopped
2 garlic cloves, crushed
24 button mushrooms, sliced
3 thyme sprigs
90 g (3¼ oz) walnuts
2 tablespoons sour cream
grated parmesan cheese, for serving

Put the porcini in a bowl with just enough boiling water to cover them and leave to soak for 30 minutes. If they soak up all the water quickly, add a little more.

Cook the penne in a large saucepan of rapidly boiling salted water until al dente. Drain well and return to the pan to keep warm.

Heat the oil in a deep frying pan and fry the onion and garlic together until translucent but not browned. Add the porcini and any soaking liquid, button mushrooms and thyme, and keep frying. The mushrooms will give off liquid as they cook so keep cooking until they soak it back up again.

In a separate pan, fry the walnuts without any oil until they start to brown and smell toasted. When they have cooled down a bit, roughly chop and add them to the mushroom mixture. Toss with the penne, stir the sour cream through and season well. Serve with the parmasen cheese.

Serves 4

# Pasta primavera

500 g (1 lb 2 oz) pasta (see Note)
155 g (5½ oz/1 cup) frozen broad
  (fava) beans
200 g (7 oz) sugar snap peas
150 g (5½ oz) asparagus spears
30 g (1 oz) butter
250 ml (9 fl oz/1 cup) pouring
  (whipping) cream
60 g (2¼ oz) grated parmesan cheese

Cook the pasta in a large saucepan
of rapidly boiling salted water until
al dente. Drain well and return to the
pan to keep warm.

Cook the beans in boiling water for
2 minutes, then refresh in iced water
and drain. Remove the skins from the
beans—you can usually just squeeze
them out, otherwise carefully slit the
skins first.

Trim the stalks from the peas and
snap the tough woody ends from the
asparagus spears. Cut the asparagus
into short lengths.

Melt the butter in a frying pan. Add
the vegetables, cream and parmesan.
Simmer gently for 3–4 minutes,
or until the peas and asparagus
are just tender. Season to taste.
Pour the sauce over the warm pasta
and toss gently. Serve immediately.

Serves 4

Note: Traditionally, primavera sauce is
served with spaghetti. We have shown
it with farfalle.

## Penne with veal ragù

2 onions, sliced
2 bay leaves, crushed
1.5 kg (3 lb 5 oz) veal shin
   (osso buco), cut into 3–4 cm
   (1¼–1½ inch) thick pieces
250 ml (9 fl oz/1 cup) dry red wine
800 g (1 lb 12 oz) tinned chopped
   tomatoes
375 m (13 fl oz/1½ cups) beef stock
2 teaspoons chopped rosemary
400 g (14 oz) penne
155 g (5½ oz/1 cup) frozen peas

Preheat the oven to 220°C (425°F/ Gas 7). Scatter the onion over the bottom of a large flameproof roasting tin, lightly spray with oil, place the bay leaves and veal pieces on top and season. Roast for 10–15 minutes, or until the veal is browned. Take care that the onion doesn't burn.

Pour the wine over the veal and return to the oven for a further 5 minutes. Reduce the heat to 180°C (350°F/Gas 4) and add the tomato, stock and 1 teaspoon of the rosemary to the tin. Cover with foil and return to the oven. Cook for 2 hours, or until the veal is starting to fall from the bone. Remove the foil and cook for a further 15 minutes, or until the meat loosens more from the bone and the liquid has evaporated slightly.

Cook the pasta in a large saucepan of rapidly boiling salted water until al dente. Drain well and return to the pan to keep warm.

Meanwhile, remove the veal from the oven and cool slightly. Add the peas and remaining rosemary and cook over medium heat for 5 minutes, or until the peas are cooked. Serve the pasta topped with the ragù.

Serves 4

## Farfalle with spinach and bacon

400 g (14 oz) farfalle
2 tablespoons extra virgin olive oil
250 g (9 oz) bacon, chopped
1 red onion, finely chopped
250 g (9 oz) baby spinach leaves
1–2 tablespoons sweet chilli sauce
30 g (1 oz/1/4 cup) crumbled feta
  cheese

Cook the pasta in a large saucepan of rapidly boiling salted water until al dente. Drain well and return to the pan to keep warm.

Meanwhile, heat the oil in a frying pan, add the bacon and cook over medium heat for 3 minutes, or until golden. Add the onion and cook for a further 4 minutes, or until softened. Toss the spinach leaves through the onion and bacon mixture for 30 seconds, or until the leaves are just wilted.

Add the bacon and spinach mixture to the pasta, then stir in the sweet chilli sauce. Season and spoon into warm pasta bowls and scatter with the crumbled feta. Serve immediately.

Serves 4

# Penne with chicken, asparagus and goat's cheese

500 g (1 lb 2 oz) penne
350 g (12 oz) asparagus spears
1 tablespoon olive oil
2 chicken breast fillets,
    cut into small cubes
1 tablespoon finely chopped thyme
250 ml (9 fl oz/1 cup) chicken stock
80 ml (2½ fl oz/⅓ cup) balsamic
    vinegar
150 g (5½ oz/1¼ cups) goat's
    cheese, crumbled

Cook the pasta in a large saucepan of rapidly boiling salted water until al dente. Drain well and return to the pan to keep warm.

Remove the woody ends from the asparagus, cut into short lengths and cook in a saucepan of boiling water for 3 minutes, or until just tender.

Heat the oil in a saucepan over high heat. Add the chicken and cook in batches, stirring occasionally, for 5 minutes, or until browned. Return all the chicken to the pan. Add the thyme and cook for 1 minute. Add the stock and vinegar and bring to the boil. Reduce the heat and simmer, stirring, for 3–4 minutes, or until the sauce has reduced slightly, then add the asparagus. Toss the pasta with the chicken and season. Sprinkle with the cheese and serve.

Serves 4

Variation: You can use feta instead of goat's cheese.

## Pasta-filled capsicum

1 tablespoon olive oil
1 onion, finely chopped
1 garlic clove, crushed
3 slices bacon, finely chopped
150 g (5½ oz) risoni, cooked
150 g (5½ oz/1 cup) grated
   mozzarella cheese
60 g (2¼ oz) grated parmesan cheese
2 tablespoons chopped flat-leaf
   (Italian) parsley
4 large red capsicum (peppers),
   halved lengthways, seeds removed
425 g (15 oz) tinned chopped
   tomatoes
125 ml (4 fl oz/½ cup) dry white wine
1 tablespoon tomato paste
   (concentrated purée)
½ teaspoon ground oregano
2 tablespoons chopped basil

Preheat the oven to 180°C (350°F/
Gas 4). Lightly grease a large shallow
ovenproof dish. Heat the oil in a frying
pan and cook the onion and garlic
over low heat until tender. Add the
bacon and stir until crisp.

Transfer to a large bowl and add the
risoni, cheeses and parsley. Spoon
into the capsicum halves and arrange
in the dish.

Combine the tomato, wine, tomato
paste and oregano. Season well,
then spoon over the risoni mixture.
Sprinkle with basil. Bake for about
35–40 minutes.

Serves 4–6

## Chicken and pasta salad

250 g (9 oz) chicken breasts fillets
375 ml (13 fl oz/1½ cups) chicken
    stock
350 g (12 oz) fusilli
150 g (5½ oz) asparagus spears,
    cut into short lengths
150 g (5½ oz) grated Gruyère cheese
2 spring onions (scallions), thinly sliced

*Dressing*
3 tablespoons olive oil
3 tablespoons lemon juice
½ teaspoon white sugar

Put the chicken and stock in a frying pan. Bring to the boil, reduce the heat and poach gently, turning regularly, for 8 minutes, or until tender. Remove, cool and thinly slice.

Cook the pasta in a large saucepan of rapidly boiling salted water until al dente. Drain well and cool.

Cook the asparagus in boiling water for 2 minutes. Drain and place in a bowl of iced water. Drain again. Combine with the chicken, pasta and cheese in a large bowl.

To make the dressing, whisk the ingredients together. Season, add to the salad and toss well. Transfer to a serving bowl and scatter with the spring onions.

Serves 4

# Minestrone primavera

3 tablespoons olive oil
45 g (1½ oz) pancetta, finely chopped
2 onions, chopped
2 garlic cloves, thinly sliced
2 small celery stalks, sliced
2 litres (70 fl oz/8 cups) chicken stock
50 g (1¾ oz/⅓ cup) macaroni
2 zucchini (courgettes), chopped
150 g (5 oz/2 cups) shredded Savoy
   cabbage
185 g (6½ oz/1½ cups) green beans,
   chopped
155 g (5 oz/1 cup) frozen peas
40 g (1¼ oz/1 cup) shredded English
   spinach leaves
1 small handful basil leaves, chopped
shredded parmesan cheese,
   for serving

Put the oil, pancetta, onion, garlic and celery in a large pan and stir occasionally over low heat for 8 minutes, or until the vegetables are soft but not brown. Add the stock and bring to the boil. Simmer, covered, for 10 minutes.

Add the macaroni and boil for 12 minutes, or until almost al dente. Stir in the zucchini, cabbage, beans and peas and simmer for 5 minutes. Add the spinach and basil and simmer for 2 minutes. Season and serve with the grated parmesan.

Serves 4–6

## Pasta shells with walnut pesto

125 g (4½ oz) day-old crusty bread, crusts removed
185 g (6½ oz/1½ cups) walnut pieces
500 g (1 lb 2 oz) small pasta shells
1 very large handful basil, roughly chopped
2–3 garlic cloves
1 small red chilli, seeded and roughly chopped
½ teaspoon finely grated lemon zest
3 tablespoons lemon juice
125 ml (4 fl oz/½ cup) olive oil

Preheat the oven to 160°C (315°F/ Gas 2–3). Cut the bread into 2 cm (¾ inch) thick slices and place on a baking tray with the walnuts. Bake for 8–10 minutes, or until the bread is dried out a little and the walnuts are lightly toasted. Don't overcook the walnuts or they will become bitter.

Meanwhile, cook the pasta in a large saucepan of rapidly boiling salted water until al dente. Drain well and return to the pan to keep warm.

Break the bread into chunks and mix in a food processor with the walnuts, basil, garlic, chilli, lemon zest and juice. Use the pulse button to chop the mixture without forming a paste. Transfer to a bowl and stir in the oil. Toss through the pasta, then season to taste with salt and pepper.

Serves 4–6

Hint: Don't add the oil to the food processor or the pesto will lose its crunchy texture.

# Pasta, bean salad with cumin and coriander dressing

300 g (10½ oz) fusilli
2 tablespoons sunflower oil
1 leek, sliced
1 red capsicum (pepper), seeded
   and diced
125 g (4½ oz) finely shredded English
   spinach
150 g (5½ oz) button mushrooms,
   halved
300 g (10½ oz) tinned red kidney
   beans, drained and rinsed
300 g (10½ oz) tinned butter beans,
   drained and rinsed
2 tablespoons snipped chives
60 g (2¼ oz) sunflower seeds, toasted

*Cumin and coriander dressing*
2 garlic cloves, crushed
½ teaspoon ground cumin
½ teaspoon ground coriander
2 tablespoons cider vinegar
125 ml (4 fl oz/½ cup) olive oil

Cook the pasta in a large saucepan of rapidly boiling salted water until al dente. Drain well and return to the pan to keep warm.

Heat the oil in a large saucepan, add the leek and capsicum and stir-fry over medium heat for 2–3 minutes. Add the spinach and mushrooms and toss together for about 1 minute, or until the spinach just wilts.

To make the dressing, mix the garlic, cumin, coriander and vinegar together. Gradually add the olive oil and whisk to combine.

Toss together the pasta, vegetables, beans, chives and ½ teaspoon of freshly ground black pepper. Toss with the dressing and sprinkle with the sunflower seeds to serve.

Serves 6

## Cavatelli with herb sauce and pecorino

400 g (14 oz) cavatelli (see Notes)
90 g (3¼ oz) butter
2 garlic cloves, crushed
3 tablespoons snipped chives
3 tablespoons shredded basil
1 tablespoon shredded sage
1 teaspoon thyme
3 tablespoons warm vegetable stock
60 g (2¼ oz) grated pecorino cheese
  (see Notes)

Cook the pasta in a large saucepan of rapidly boiling salted water until al dente. Drain well and return to the pan to keep warm.

Meanwhile, heat the butter in a small saucepan over medium heat, add the garlic and cook for 1 minute, or until fragrant. Add the herbs and cook for a further minute.

Add the herb mixture and stock to the pasta. Return to the heat for 2–3 minutes, or until warmed through. Season, add the pecorino, stir well and divide among bowls.

Serves 4

Note: Cavatelli is a short pasta with rolled edges. You can substitute small pasta shells. Pecorino is an Italian sheep's milk cheese with a sharp flavour. If you can't find it, use parmesan instead.

# Greek cheese bake

415 g (14¾ oz/2 cups) orzo
60 g (2¼ oz) butter
6 spring onions (scallions), chopped
450 g (1 lb) English spinach, chopped
2 tablespoons plain (all-purpose) flour
1.25 litres (44 fl oz/5 cups) milk
250 g (9 oz) kefalotyri cheese, grated
(see Note)
250 g (9 oz) marinated feta cheese,
drained
3 tablespoons chopped dill

Preheat the oven to 190°C (375°F/ Gas 5). Cook the pasta in a large saucepan of rapidly boiling salted water until al dente. Drain well and return to the pan keep warm. Heat 1 tablespoon of the butter in a large saucepan over high heat and cook the spring onion for 30 seconds. Add the spinach and stir for 1 minute, or until wilted. Season and stir into the pasta.

Put the remaining butter in the saucepan in which the spinach was cooked. Melt over low heat, then stir in the flour and cook for 1 minute, or until pale and foaming. Remove from the heat and gradually stir in the milk. Return to the heat and stir constantly for 5 minutes, or until the sauce boils and thickens. Add two-thirds of the kefalotyri and all of the feta and stir for 2 minutes until melted. Remove from the heat and stir in the dill.

Combine the pasta mixture with the cheese sauce, season and pour into a lightly greased 2.5 litre (87 fl oz/ 10 cup) ovenproof dish. Sprinkle the remaining cheese on top and bake for 15 minutes, or until golden.

Serves 6

Note: Kefalotyri is a hard Greek sheep's milk cheese; it is similar to parmesan.

# Farfalle salad with sun-dried tomatoes and spinach

500 g (1 lb 2 oz) farfalle or fusilli
3 spring onions (scallions), finely
  chopped
60 g (2¼ oz) sun-dried tomatoes,
  cut into strips
500 g (1 lb 2 oz) English spinach,
  shredded
50 g (1¾ oz/⅓ cup) pine nuts,
  toasted
1 tablespoon chopped oregano

*Dressing*
3 tablespoons olive oil
1 teaspoon chopped chilli
1 garlic clove, crushed

Cook the pasta in a large saucepan of rapidly boiling salted water until al dente. Drain well and rinse under cold water. Transfer to a large salad bowl. Add the spring onion, tomato, spinach, pine nuts and oregano to the pasta.

To make the dressing, put the oil, chilli and garlic in a small screw-top jar and season. Shake well.

Pour the dressing over the salad, toss well and serve immediately.

Serves 4–6

## Pasta pie

250 g (9 oz) macaroni
1 tablespoon olive oil
1 onion, sliced
125 g (4½ oz) pancetta, chopped
125 g (4½ oz) ham, chopped
4 eggs
250 ml (9 fl oz/1 cup) milk
250 ml (9 fl oz/1 cup) pouring
  (whipping) cream
2 tablespoons snipped chives
120 g (4¼ oz) grated cheddar cheese
125 g (4½ oz) bocconcini (baby
  mozzarella cheese), chopped

Preheat the oven to 180°C (350°F/ Gas 4). Cook the pasta in a large saucepan of rapidly boiling salted water until al dente. Drain well. Spread evenly over the base of a greased 2 litre (70 fl oz/8 cup) ovenproof dish.

Heat the oil in a large frying pan and cook the onion over low heat until tender. Add the pancetta and cook for 2 minutes. Add the ham and stir well. Remove from the heat to cool.

Whisk together the eggs, milk, cream, chives and season. Add the cheddar cheese, chopped bocconcini and the pancetta mixture and stir well. Spread evenly over the macaroni. Bake for 35–40 minutes, or until set.

Serves 4

# Rigatoni with tomato, haloumi and spinach

6 Roma (plum) tomatoes
white sugar, for sprinkling
4 garlic cloves, chopped
40 g (13 oz) rigatoni
3 tablespoons lemon juice
3 tablespoons olive oil
200 g (7 oz) haloumi cheese,
   thinly sliced
100 g (3½ oz) baby spinach leaves

Preheat the oven to 180°C (350°F/ Gas 4). Put the tomatoes on a baking tray, lined with foil, and sprinkle generously with sugar, salt, pepper and garlic. Bake for 1 hour, or until quite dehydrated and shrunken. Allow to cool. Cut in half.

Meanwhile, cook the pasta in a large pan of rapidly boiling salted water until al dente. Drain, rinse under cold water and drain again. Allow to cool.

Combine the lemon juice and olive oil and season.

Toss the lemon dressing though the pasta. Lightly toss the tomato, haloumi cheese and spinach through.

Serves 6

## Gnocchi cheese bake

500 g (1 lb 2 oz) fresh potato gnocchi
30 g (1 oz) butter, chopped
1 tablespoon chopped flat-leaf (Italian)
  parsley
100 g (3½ oz) fontina cheese, sliced
100 g (3½ oz) provolone cheese,
  sliced

Preheat the oven to 200°C (400°F/ Gas 6). Cook the gnocchi, in batches, in a large saucepan of boiling water for about 2 minutes, or until the gnocchi rise to the surface. Carefully remove from the pan with a slotted spoon and drain well.

Put the gnocchi in a lightly greased ovenproof dish. Scatter with the butter and parsley. Lay the cheeses over the top, season and bake for 10 minutes until the cheese has melted.

Serves 4

## Grilled capsicum and anchovy salad

500 g (1 lb 2 oz) penne or fusilli
2 large red capsicum (peppers)
1 small onion, finely chopped
2 large handfuls flat-leaf (Italian)
   parsley leaves
2 anchovies, whole or chopped
3 tablespoons olive oil
2 tablespoons lemon juice

Cook the pasta in a large saucepan of rapidly boiling salted water until al dente. Drain and rinse under cold water.

Cut the capsicum into large pieces, removing the seeds and membrane. Place, skin side up, under a hot grill (broiler) and cook for 8 minutes, or until the skin is blistered and black. Cool in a plastic bag, then peel away the skin and cut the flesh into thin strips.

Toss together the pasta, capsicum, onion, parsley, anchovies, oil and lemon juice and season. Serve immediately.

Serves 4–6

Hint: The capsicum can be grilled and peeled a day in advance, covered well and then refrigerated. Removing the skin in this way results in a much sweeter taste.

# Sweet potato and prosciutto penne

500 g (1 lb 2 oz) penne
500 g (1 lb 2 oz) orange sweet potato,
   diced
2 tablespoons extra virgin olive oil
5 spring onions (scallions), sliced
2 small garlic cloves, crushed
8 thin slices prosciutto, chopped
125 g (4½ oz) sun-dried tomatoes in
   oil, drained and sliced
1 small handful basil leaves, shredded
crusty bread, to serve

Cook the penne in a large saucepan of rapidly boiling salted water until al dente. Drain well and return to the pan to keep warm.

Meanwhile, steam the sweet potato for 5 minutes, or until tender. Heat the oil in a saucepan, add the spring onion, garlic and sweet potato and stir over medium heat for 2–3 minutes, or until the spring onion is soft. Add the prosciutto and tomato and cook for a further 1 minute.

Add the sweet potato mixture to the penne and toss over low heat until heated through. Add the basil and season with freshly ground black pepper. Serve immediately with bread.

Serves 4

## Cajun scallops with pasta and buttery corn sauce

350 g (11 oz) small pasta shells
20 large scallops, without roe
2 tablespoons Cajun spice mix
2 tablespoons corn oil
250 g (8 oz) butter
3 garlic cloves, crushed
400 g (13 oz) tinned corn kernels, drained
60 ml (2 fl oz/¼ cup) lime juice
4 tablespoons finely chopped fresh coriander (cilantro) leaves

Cook the pasta in a large pan of rapidly boiling salted water until al dente. Drain and return to the pan to keep warm. Meanwhile, pat the scallops dry with paper towel and lightly coat in the spice mix. Heat the oil in a large frying pan and cook the scallops for 1 minute each side over high heat (ensuring they are well spaced), then remove from the pan, cover and keep warm.

Reduce the heat to medium, add the butter and cook for 4 minutes, or until foaming and golden brown. Remove from the heat, add the garlic, corn and lime juice. Gently toss the corn mixture through the pasta with 2 tablespoons of coriander and season well. Divide among four serving plates, top with the scallops, drizzle with any juices and sprinkle with the remaining coriander.

Notes: Scallops should not be crowded when they are cooked or they will release all their juices, causing them to stew and toughen. To really achieve the most delicious flavours, don't use a non-stick frying pan—they can prevent the butter from properly browning and the juices from caramelising.

Serves 4

# Pesto beef salad

1 large yellow capsicum (pepper)
1 large red capsicum (pepper)
100 g (3½ oz) lean fillet steak
125 g (4½ oz/1½ cups) penne
100 g (3½ oz) button mushrooms,
    quartered

*Pesto*
2 large handfuls basil leaves
2 garlic cloves, chopped
2 tablespoons pepitas (pumpkin
    seeds)
1 tablespoon olive oil
2 tablespoons orange juice
1 tablespoon lemon juice

Cut the capsicum into quarters, discarding the seeds and membrane. Grill (broil) the capsicum, skin side up, until the skins blacken and blister. Cool under a damp tea towel, then peel and dice the flesh.

Spray a non-stick frying pan with oil and cook the steak over high heat for 3–4 minutes each side. Remove and leave for 5 minutes before cutting into thin slices. Season with a little salt.

To make the pesto, place the basil leaves, garlic and pepitas in a food processor and finely chop. With the motor running, add the oil, orange and lemon juice and season well.

Meanwhile, cook the pasta in a large saucepan of rapidly boiling salted water until al dente. Drain well and toss with the pesto in a large bowl.

Add the capsicum, steak and mushroom to the penne and toss to distribute evenly. Serve immediately.

*Serves 4*

# Four-cheese macaroni

450 g (1 lb) elbow macaroni
2 tablespoons butter, chopped
300 ml (10 fl oz) pouring
(whipping) cream
125 g (4½ oz) fontina cheese, sliced
125 g (4½ oz/1¼ cup) grated
provolone cheese
100 g (3½ oz/¾ cup) grated Gruyère
cheese
125 g (4½ oz) blue castello cheese,
crumbled
40 g (1½ oz/½ cup) fresh
breadcrumbs
3 tablespoons grated parmesan
cheese

Preheat the oven to 180°C (350°F/
Gas 4). Cook the pasta in a large
saucepan of rapidly boiling salted
water until al dente. Drain well and
return to the pan to keep warm.

Melt half the butter in a large
saucepan. Add the cream and,
when just coming to the boil, add the
fontina, provolone, Gruyère and blue
cheeses, stirring constantly over low
heat for 3 minutes, or until melted.
Season, add the pasta to the cheese
mixture and mix well.

Spoon the mixture into a greased
shallow 2 litre (70 fl oz/8 cup)
ovenproof dish. Sprinkle with
the combined breadcrumbs and
parmesan, dot with the butter and
bake for 25 minutes, or until the top
is golden and crisp.

Serves 4

# Warm pesto and prawn salad

500 g (1 lb 2 oz) elbow macaroni
150 g (5½ oz) capers in brine, drained,
    rinsed and patted dry
3 tablespoons olive oil
2 tablespoons extra virgin olive oil
2 garlic cloves, chopped
2 tomatoes, seeded and diced
150 g (5½ oz) thin asparagus,
    trimmed, halved and blanched
2 tablespoons balsamic vinegar
150 g (5½ oz) rocket (arugula)
20 cooked prawns (shrimp), peeled,
    tails intact
shaved parmesan cheese, for serving

*Pesto*
2 garlic cloves, crushed
1 teaspoon salt
40 g (1½ oz/¼ cup) pine nuts, toasted
2 large handfuls basil leaves
60 g (2¼ oz) grated parmesan cheese
3 tablespoons extra virgin olive oil

To make the pesto, blend the garlic, salt, pine nuts, basil leaves and grated parmesan in a food processor or blender until thoroughly combined. With the motor running, add the oil in a thin steady stream and process until the pesto is smooth.

Cook the pasta in a large saucepan of rapidly boiling salted water until al dente. Drain well, transfer to a large bowl and toss the pesto through.

Heat the olive oil in a frying pan and fry the capers for 4–5 minutes, stirring occasionally, until crisp. Drain on paper towels.

Heat the extra virgin olive oil in a deep frying pan over medium heat and add the garlic, tomatoes and asparagus. Toss continuously for 1–2 minutes, or until warmed through. Stir in the balsamic vinegar.

When the pasta is just warm, not hot (or it will wilt the rocket), toss the tomato mixture, rocket and prawns with the pasta and season. Serve scattered with capers and parmesan.

Serves 4

## Ham and cheese pasta bake

1½ tablespoons olive oil
1 onion, finely chopped
300 g (10½ oz) leg ham, sliced
3 mm (⅛ inch) thick and cut
into 5 cm (2 inch) lengths
600 ml (21 fl oz) pouring
(whipping) cream
300 g (10½ oz) peas
375 g (13 oz) small pasta shells
3 tablespoons chopped basil
250 g (9 oz/2 cups) grated mature
cheddar cheese

Preheat the oven to 200°C (400°F/
Gas 6) and lightly grease a 2.5 litre
(87.5 fl oz/10 cup) ovenproof dish.
Heat 1 tablespoon of the oil in a frying
pan over medium heat and cook the
onion, stirring frequently for 5 minutes,
or until soft. Add the remaining oil,
then the ham and cook, stirring, for
1 minute. Pour the cream into the
pan, bring to the boil, then reduce
the heat and simmer for 6 minutes.
Add the peas and cook for another
2–4 minutes, or until the mixture
has reduced and thickened slightly.
Season.

Meanwhile, cook the pasta in a large
saucepan of rapidly boiling salted
water until al dente. Drain and return
to the pan to keep warm.

Add the cream sauce to the pasta,
then the basil and three-quarters of
the cheese. Stir well and season.
Transfer the mixture to the prepared
dish, sprinkle on the remaining cheese
and bake for 20 minutes, or until the
top is golden brown.

Serves 4

Filled

## Pasta shells stuffed with roasted pumpkin and ricotta

1 kg (2 lb 4 oz) butternut pumpkin
  (winter squash), cut into large
  wedges
olive oil, to drizzle
10 garlic cloves, unpeeled
500 g (1 lb 2 oz/2 cups) ricotta cheese
1 handful basil leaves, shredded
750 ml (26 fl oz/3 cups) Italian
  tomato pasta sauce
125 ml (4 fl oz/½ cup) dry white wine
56 pasta shells (or 32 large
  pasta shells)
100 g (3½ oz/1 cup) grated
  parmesan cheese

Preheat the oven to 200°C (400°F/
Gas 6). Place the pumpkin in a baking
dish, drizzle with oil and season. Bake
for 30 minutes, then add the garlic
and bake for 15 minutes, or until
tender. Cool slightly, then peel and
mash the pumpkin and garlic. Mix
with the ricotta and half the basil
and season.

Put the pasta sauce and wine in
a saucepan, bring to the boil, then
reduce the heat and simmer for
10 minutes, or until slightly thickened.

Cook the pasta in a large saucepan
of rapidly boiling salted water until al
dente. Drain well and lay out on a tea
towel to dry, then fill with the pumpkin
mixture. Spread any remaining filling
in a large ovenproof dish, top with
the shells and pour on the sauce.
Sprinkle with parmesan and the
remaining basil and bake for about
15–20 minutes (or 30 minutes for
the giant shells).

Serves 6

## Lemon-scented broth with tortellini

1 lemon
125 ml (4 fl oz/½ cup) dry white wine
500 ml (17 fl oz/2 cups) tinned
  chicken consommé
1 very large handful chopped flat-leaf
  (Italian) parsley leaves
375 g (13 oz) fresh veal- or chicken-
  tortellini

Using a vegetable peeler, peel wide strips from the lemon. Remove the white pith with a small sharp knife and cut three of the wide lemon pieces into thin strips. Set these aside for garnishing.

Place the wide lemon strips, wine, consommé and 750 ml (26 fl oz/ 3 cups) water in a large deep saucepan. Cook for 10 minutes over low heat. Remove the lemon strips and bring to the boil.

Add half the parsley, the tortellini and a sprinkling of black pepper to the pan. Cook for 6–7 minutes or until the pasta is al dente. Garnish with the remaining parsley and the thin strips of lemon.

Serves 4–6

# Spinach and ricotta ravioli

1 tablespoon olive oil
1 red onion, finely chopped
1 garlic clove, crushed
200 g (7 oz) baby spinach leaves,
    coarsely chopped
250 g (9 oz/1 cup) ricotta cheese
2 egg yolks, lightly beaten
2 tablespoons grated parmesan
    cheese
freshly grated nutmeg, to taste
48 won ton wrappers
2 tablespoons butter
2 tablespoons sage leaves

Heat the oil in a frying pan, add the onion and garlic and fry over low heat for a few minutes until the onion is soft and translucent. Add the spinach and stir around until it wilts.

Stir the spinach mixture into the ricotta, along with the egg yolk, parmesan and season with nutmeg, salt and pepper.

Brush a little water around the edge of a won ton wrapper and put a teaspoon of filling in the centre. Fold the wrapper over to make a half moon shape and press the edges firmly together. Put the ravioli on a tea towel and repeat with the remaining wrappers.

Bring a large saucepan of water to the boil and cook the ravioli for a few minutes. They will float to the surface when ready. Scoop out carefully with a slotted spoon and drain in a colander.

Melt the butter in a small saucepan, add the sage and sizzle for a few minutes until the butter browns slightly. Put the ravioli in bowls and pour the sage butter over.

Serves 4

## Agnolotti with salmon, capers and brown butter

125 ml (4 fl oz/1/2 cup) olive oil
100 g (31/2 oz) capers in brine,
    drained, rinsed and patted dry
500 g (1 lb 2 oz) salmon fillets,
    skinned
625 g (1 lb 6 oz) fresh ricotta agnolotti
150 g (51/2 oz) butter
11/2 teaspoons grated lemon zest
2 tablespoons lemon juice
3 tablespoons chopped flat-leaf
    (Italian) parsley

Heat half the oil in a small frying pan and cook the capers over high heat for 3–4 minutes, until golden and crispy. Drain on paper towels.

Season the salmon fillets on both sides. Heat the remaining oil in a non-stick frying pan and cook the salmon for 2–3 minutes each side, or until just cooked through but still pink in the centre. Remove from the pan and keep warm. Flake with your fingers.

Cook the pasta in a large saucepan of rapidly boiling salted water until al dente. Drain well and return to the pan to keep warm.

Heat the butter in a frying pan over low heat for 5 minutes, or until golden. Add the lemon zest, juice and parsley. Top the pasta with the flaked salmon and pour on the brown butter. Scatter with the capers and serve immediately.

Serves 4

## Tortellini boscaiola

30 g (1 oz) butter
4 slices bacon, chopped
2 garlic cloves, crushed
1 small leek, thinly sliced
300 g (10½ oz) Swiss brown or button
  mushrooms, sliced
3 tablespoons dry white wine
375 ml (13 fl oz/1½ cups) pouring
  (whipping) cream
1 teaspoon chopped thyme
500 g (1 lb 2 oz) fresh veal tortellini
50 g (1¾ oz/½ cup) grated
  parmesan cheese
1 tablespoon chopped flat-leaf (Italian)
  parsley

Melt the butter in a large frying pan, add the bacon and cook over medium heat for 5 minutes, or until crisp. Add the garlic and leek, and cook for 2 minutes, then add the mushrooms and cook for 8 minutes, or until softened. Add the wine, cream and thyme, bring to the boil, then reduce the heat and simmer for 10 minutes, or until the sauce has thickened.

Meanwhile, cook the tortellini in a large saucepan of rapidly boiling salted water until al dente. Drain well. Add the parmesan to the sauce and stir over low heat until melted. Season. Combine the sauce with the tortellini and parsley.

Serves 4–6

## Veal agnolotti with alfredo sauce

625 g (1 lb 6 oz) fresh veal agnolotti
90 g (3¼ oz) butter
150 g (5½ oz/1½ cups) grated
  parmesan cheese
300 ml (10½ fl oz) pouring
  (whipping) cream
2 tablespoons chopped marjoram

Cook the veal agnolotti in a large saucepan of rapidly boiling salted water until al dente. Drain and return to the pan to keep warm.

Just before the pasta is cooked, melt the butter in a saucepan over low heat. Add the parmesan and cream and bring to the boil. Reduce the heat and simmer, stirring constantly, for 2 minutes, or until the sauce has thickened slightly. Stir in the marjoram and season. Toss the sauce through the pasta. Serve immediately.

Serves 4–6

Note: Any fresh herb such as flat-leaf (Italian) parsley, thyme, chervil or dill can be used instead of marjoram.

# Ravioli with herbs

2 tablespoons olive oil
1 garlic clove, halved
800 g (1 lb 12 oz) fresh ravioli
60 g (2¼ oz) butter, chopped
2 tablespoons chopped flat-leaf
  (Italian) parsley
1 large handful basil leaves, chopped
2 tablespoons snipped chives

Combine the oil and garlic in a small bowl and set aside.

Cook the pasta in a large saucepan of rapidly boiling salted water until al dente. Drain well and return to the pan to keep warm.

Strain the garlic oil and add to the pasta, discarding the garlic. Add the butter and herbs and toss well.

Serves 4–6

Variation: Use fresh coriander (cilantro) instead of parsley.

## Veal tortellini with creamy mushroom sauce

500 g (1 lb 2 oz) fresh veal tortellini
3 tablespoons olive oil
600 g (1 lb 5 oz) Swiss brown
  mushrooms, thinly sliced
2 garlic cloves, crushed
125 ml (4 fl oz/½ cup) dry white wine
300 ml (10½ fl oz) thick
  (double/heavy) cream
pinch ground nutmeg
3 tablespoons finely chopped flat-leaf
  (Italian) parsley
30 g (1 oz/⅓ cup) grated
  parmesan cheese

Cook the pasta in a large saucepan of rapidly boiling salted water until al dente. Drain well and return to the pan to keep warm

Meanwhile, heat the oil in a frying pan over medium heat. Add the mushrooms and cook, stirring occasionally, for 5 minutes, or until softened. Add the garlic and cook for 1 minute, then stir in the wine and cook for 5 minutes, or until the liquid has reduced by half.

Combine the cream, nutmeg and parsley, add to the sauce and cook for 3–5 minutes, or until the sauce thickens slightly. Season. Divide the tortellini among serving plates and spoon on the mushroom sauce. Sprinkle with parmesan and serve.

Serves 4

## Roasted vegetable cannelloni

60 g (2¼ oz) butter
1 large leek, cut into 1 cm
  (½ inch) pieces
200 g (7 oz) chargrilled eggplant
  (aubergine) in oil, cut into 1 cm
  (½ inch) pieces
200 g (7 oz) chargrilled orange sweet
  potato in oil, cut into 1 cm
  (½ inch) pieces
125 g (4½ oz/1 cup) grated
  cheddar cheese
50 g (1¾ oz/⅓ cup) plain
  (all-purpose) flour
1 litre (35 fl oz/4 cups) milk
6 fresh lasagne sheets

Preheat the oven to 200°C (400°F/ Gas 6) and lightly grease a 28 cm x 18 cm x 5 cm (11¼ inch x 7 inch x 2 inch) ovenproof dish. Melt one-third of the butter in a saucepan, add the leek and stir over medium heat for 8 minutes, or until soft. Mix the eggplant, sweet potato, leek and one-third of the cheddar.

Melt the remaining butter in a saucepan over medium heat. Stir in the flour and cook for 1 minute, or until foaming. Remove from the heat and gradually stir in the milk. Return to the heat and stir until the sauce boils and thickens. Reduce the heat and simmer for 2 minutes. Season and stir 375 ml (13 fl oz/1½ cups) of the sauce into the vegetable mixture, adding extra if necessary to bind.

Cut the lasagne sheets in half widthways. Spoon vegetable mixture along the centre of one sheet and roll up. Repeat to make 12 tubes.

Place the tubes, seam side down, in the dish and spoon the remaining white sauce over the top to cover. Sprinkle with the remaining cheese and bake for about 20 minutes, or until the cheese is golden.

Serves 4

## Ravioli with roasted red capsicum sauce

6 red capsicum (peppers)
625 g (1 lb 6 oz) fresh ravioli
2 tablespoons olive oil
3 garlic cloves, crushed
2 leeks, thinly sliced
1 tablespoon chopped oregano
2 teaspoons soft brown sugar
250 ml (9 fl oz/1 cup) hot vegetable
  or chicken stock

Cut the capsicum into large pieces, removing the seeds and membrane. Cook, skin side up, under a hot grill (broiler) until the skin blackens and blisters. Cool in a plastic bag, then peel away the skin.

Cook the pasta in a large saucepan of rapidly boiling salted water until al dente. Drain well and return to the pan to keep warm

Meanwhile, heat the oil in a frying pan and cook the garlic and leek over medium heat for 3–4 minutes, or until softened. Add the oregano and brown sugar and stir for 1 minute.

Place the capsicum and leek mixture in a food processor or blender, season and process until combined. Add the stock and process until smooth.

Gently toss the sauce through the ravioli over low heat until warmed through. Divide among serving bowls and serve immediately.

Serves 4

## Veal tortellini with roasted pumpkin and basil butter

1 kg (2 lb 4 oz) jap pumpkin
  (winter squash), cut into
  2 cm (¾ inch) cubes
600 g (1 lb 5 oz) fresh veal tortellini
100 g (3½ oz) butter
3 garlic cloves, crushed
80 g (2¾ oz/½ cup) pine nuts
1 handful basil leaves, shredded
200 g (7 oz) feta cheese, crumbled

Preheat the oven to 220°C (425°F/ Gas 7). Line a baking tray with baking paper. Place the pumpkin on the prepared tray and season. Bake for 30 minutes, or until tender.

Meanwhile, cook the pasta in a large saucepan of boiling salted water until al dente. Drain and return to the pan.

Heat the butter over medium heat in a small frying pan until foaming. Add the garlic and pine nuts and cook for 3–5 minutes, or until the nuts are starting to turn golden. Remove from the heat and add the basil. Toss the basil butter, pumpkin and feta through the cooked pasta and serve.

Serves 4

## Herb-filled ravioli

300 g (10½ oz) plain (all-purpose) flour
4 eggs, lightly beaten
3 tablespoons olive oil
250 g (9 oz/1 cup) ricotta cheese
2 tablespoons grated parmesan
cheese
2 teaspoons snipped chives
1 tablespoon chopped flat-leaf (Italian)
parsley
2 teaspoons chopped basil
1 teaspoon chopped lemon thyme
or thyme

Sift the flour into a bowl and make a well in the centre. Gradually mix in three-quarters of the eggs and all of the oil. Turn out onto a lightly floured surface and knead for 6 minutes, or until elastic. Cover with plastic wrap and leave for 30 minutes.

To make the filling, mix the ricotta, parmesan and herbs. Season well.

Divide the dough into four portions and shape each into a log. Keep unworked portions covered. Roll out each portion as thinly as possible into rectangles, making two portions slightly larger and wider than the other two.

Lay one of the smaller sheets out. Spoon 1 teaspoon of the filling at 5 cm (2 inch) intervals. Brush with the remaining egg between the filling along the cutting lines. Place a larger sheet on top. Press the two sheets together along the cutting lines. Cut the ravioli with a pastry cutter or knife. Transfer to a lightly floured baking tray. Repeat with the remaining sheets and filling. Cook the ravioli in a large saucepan of rapidly boiling water for 5–8 minutes and top with a sauce of your choice.

Serves 4

# Roasted chunky ratatouille cannelloni

1 eggplant (aubergine)
2 zucchini (courgettes)
1 large red capsicum (pepper)
1 large green capsicum (pepper)
3–4 ripe Roma (plum) tomatoes
12 garlic cloves, unpeeled
3 tablespoons olive oil
300 ml (10½ fl oz) Italian tomato
  pasta sauce
350 g (12 oz) cannelloni tubes
3 tablespoons shredded basil
300 g (10½ oz) ricotta cheese
100 g (3½ oz) feta cheese
1 egg, lightly beaten
50 g (1¾ oz) grated pecorino cheese

Preheat the oven to 200°C (400°F/ Gas 6). Cut the eggplant, zucchini, capsicum and tomatoes into 2 cm (¾ inch) cubes and place in a baking dish with the garlic. Drizzle with the oil and toss to coat. Bake for 1½ hours, or until the vegetables are tender and the tomatoes slightly mushy. Peel and lightly mash the garlic cloves.

Pour the tomato sauce over the base of a large ovenproof dish. Spoon the ratatouille into the cannelloni tubes and arrange in the dish.

Combine the basil, ricotta, feta and egg, season well and spoon over the cannelloni. Sprinkle with the pecorino and bake for 30 minutes, or until the cannelloni are soft.

Serves 6–8

## Ham tortellini with nutty herb sauce

500 g (1 lb 2 oz) fresh ham and
 cheese tortellini
60 g (2¼ oz) butter
125 g (4½ oz/1 cup) walnuts,
 chopped
100 g (3½ oz/²/₃ cup) pine nuts
2 tablespoons finely chopped flat-leaf
 (Italian) parsley
2 teaspoons chopped thyme
3 tablespoons ricotta cheese
3 tablespoons pouring
 (whipping) cream

Cook the pasta in a large saucepan
of rapidly boiling salted water until
al dente. Drain well and return to the
pan to keep warm.

Meanwhile, heat the butter in a frying
pan over medium heat until foaming.
Add the walnuts and pine nuts and
stir for 5 minutes, or until golden
brown. Add the parsley and thyme
and season.

Beat the ricotta and cream together.
Add the nutty sauce, then stir through
the pasta. Divide among bowls.

Serves 4–6

## Salmon and ricotta-stuffed pasta shells

200 g (7 oz) pasta shells
425 g (15 oz) tinned red salmon,
  drained, bones removed and flaked
500 g (1 lb 2 oz) ricotta cheese
1 tablespoon chopped flat-leaf
  (Italian) parsley
3 tablespoons chopped chives
1½ celery stalks, finely chopped
90 g (3¼ oz/¾ cup) grated cheddar
  cheese
185 ml (6 fl oz/¾ cup) pouring
  (whipping) cream
3 tablespoons grated parmesan
  cheese

Preheat the oven to 180°C (350°F/ Gas 4). Cook the pasta in a large saucepan of boiling salted water until al dente. Drain well and return to the pan to keep warm.

Combine the salmon, ricotta, parsley, chives, celery and cheddar in a large bowl and season. Put 2 teaspoons of filling in each shell. Place the filled shells into a 3 litre (105 fl oz/12 cup) ovenproof dish.

Pour over the cream and sprinkle with the parmesan. Cover with foil and bake for 20 minutes, then remove the foil and bake for a further 15 minutes, or until golden brown. Spoon the cream sauce over the shells to serve.

Serves 4

## Beetroot ravioli with sage burnt butter sauce

340 g (12 oz) baby beetroots
  in sweet vinegar
40 g (1½ oz) grated parmesan cheese
250 g (9 oz/1 cup) ricotta cheese
750 g (1 lb 10 oz) fresh lasagne sheets
  (4 sheets)
fine polenta, for sprinkling
200 g (7 oz) butter, chopped
1 very small handful sage leaves, torn
2 garlic cloves, crushed
shaved parmesan cheese, for serving

Drain the beetroot, then grate it into a bowl. Add the parmesan and ricotta and mix well. Lay a sheet of pasta on a flat surface and place 12 evenly spaced tablespoons of the ricotta mixture on the pasta—four across and three down. Flatten the mounds of filling slightly. Lightly brush the edges of the pasta sheet and around each pile of filling with water.

Place a second sheet of pasta over the top and gently press around each mound to seal and enclose the filling. Using a pasta cutter or sharp knife, cut the pasta into 12 ravioli. Lay them out separately on a lined tray that has been sprinkled with polenta. Gently remove any air bubbles after cutting so that they are completely sealed. Repeat with the remaining filling and lasagne sheets.

Cook the pasta in a large saucepan of boiling water until al dente. Drain, divide among serving plates and keep warm. Melt the butter in a saucepan and cook for 3–4 minutes, or until golden brown. Remove from the heat, stir in the sage and garlic and spoon over the ravioli. Scatter with shaved parmesan and season.

Serves 4

## Tortellini with speck, asparagus and tomato

200 g (7 oz) piece speck (skin
  removed), roughly chopped
4 tomatoes
310 g (11 oz) asparagus, cut into
  3 cm (1 1/4 inch) lengths
500 g (1 lb 2 oz) fresh cheese tortellini
1 tablespoon olive oil
1 red onion, thinly sliced
1 tablespoon tomato paste
  (concentrated purée)
125 ml (4 fl oz/1/2 cup) chicken stock
2 teaspoons thyme leaves

Put the speck in a food processor
and pulse until chopped.

Score a cross in the base of the
tomatoes. Put in a heatproof bowl
and cover with boiling water. Leave
for 30 seconds, then transfer to cold
water and peel the skin away from
the cross. Roughly chop.

Cook the asparagus in a large
saucepan of boiling water for
2 minutes, or until just tender.
Remove with a slotted spoon and
refresh in cold water. Drain. Cook the
pasta in the same boiling water and
cook until al dente. Drain well and
return to the pan to keep warm.

Meanwhile, heat the oil in a saucepan
over medium heat. Add the speck
and onion and cook, stirring, for
2–3 minutes, or until the onion is soft.
Add the tomato, tomato paste, stock
and thyme and season. Cook, stirring,
for 5 minutes. Add the pasta and
asparagus to the tomato mixture
and stir over low heat until warmed
through.

Serves 4–6

## Chicken ravioli with fresh tomato sauce

*Tomato sauce*
1 tablespoon olive oil
1 large onion, chopped
2 garlic cloves, crushed
90 g (3¼ oz/⅓ cup) tomato paste
  (concentrated purée)
3 tablespoons dry red wine
170 ml (5½ fl oz/⅔ cup) chicken
  stock
2 tomatoes, chopped
1 tablespoon chopped basil

*Ravioli*
200 g (7 oz) minced (ground) chicken
1 tablespoon chopped basil
3 tablespoons grated parmesan
  cheese
3 spring onions (scallions), finely
  chopped
50 g (1¾ oz) ricotta cheese
48 round won ton or gow gee
  wrappers

To make the tomato sauce, heat the oil in a saucepan and cook the onion and garlic for 2–3 minutes, then stir in the tomato paste, wine, stock and tomato and simmer for 20 minutes. Stir in the basil.

To make the ravioli, combine the chicken, basil, parmesan, spring onion, ricotta and season. Lay 24 wrappers on a flat surface and brush with a little water. Place slightly heaped teaspoons of the mixture onto the centre of each wrapper. Place another wrapper on top and press the edges together.

Bring a large saucepan of salted water to the boil. Add the ravioli, a few at a time, and cook for 2–3 minutes, or until just tender. Drain well and serve with the tomato sauce.

Serves 4

## Agnolotti with creamy semi-dried tomato sauce and bacon

4 slices bacon
625 g (1 lb 6 oz) fresh veal or chicken
  agnolotti
1 tablespoon olive oil
2 garlic cloves, finely chopped
110 g (3¾ oz/⅔ cup) thinly sliced
  semi-dried (sun-blushed) tomatoes
1 tablespoon chopped thyme
375 ml (13 fl oz/1½ cups) pouring
  (whipping) cream
1 teaspoon finely grated lemon zest
35 g (1¼ oz/⅓ cup) grated
  parmesan cheese

Grill (broil) the bacon for 5 minutes each side, or until crisp and golden. Drain well on paper towel, then break into pieces.

Cook the pasta in a large saucepan of rapidly boiling salted water until al dente. Drain well and return to the pan to keep warm.

Heat the oil in a frying pan over medium heat. Cook the garlic for 1 minute, or until just golden. Add the tomato and thyme and cook for a further 1 minute.

Add the cream, bring to the boil, then reduce the heat and simmer for about 6–8 minutes, or until the cream has thickened and reduced by one-third. Season and add the lemon zest and two-thirds of the parmesan. Pour the sauce over the pasta and coat well. Divide among bowls, sprinkle with the remaining parmesan and the bacon pieces.

Serves 4

## Quick mushroom and ricotta cannelloni

500 g (1 lb 2 oz) button mushrooms
200 g (7 oz) fresh lasagne sheets
2 tablespoons olive oil
3 garlic cloves, crushed
2 tablespoons lemon juice
400 g (14 oz) ricotta cheese
3 tablespoons chopped basil
425 ml (15 fl oz) Italian tomato
   pasta sauce
150 g (5½ oz/1 cup) grated
   mozzarella cheese

Preheat the oven to 180°C (350°F/ Gas 4). Finely chop the mushrooms in a food processor. Cut the lasagne sheets into twelve 13 cm x 16 cm (5 inch x 6¼ inch) rectangles.

Heat the oil in a large frying pan over medium heat. Add the garlic and mushrooms and cook, stirring, for 3 minutes. Add the lemon juice and cook for a further 2 minutes, or until the mushrooms are softened. Transfer to a sieve over a bowl to collect the juices, pressing with a spoon to remove as much moisture as possible. Reserve.

Place the mushrooms in a bowl with the ricotta and basil. Season generously and mix well. Take a lasagne sheet and place heaped tablespoons of the mixture along one long edge. Roll up and arrange in a single layer in a greased 2 litre (70 fl oz/8 cup) shallow ovenproof dish. Repeat with the remaining mixture and lasagne sheets. Pour on the reserved mushroom cooking liquid then pour on the pasta sauce. Sprinkle with mozzarella cheese and bake for 25 minutes, or until golden and bubbling.

Serves 4

## Baked shells with ricotta and prosciutto

24 large pasta shells
200 g (7 oz) prosciutto, roughly
  chopped
2 tablespoons snipped chives
2 very large handfuls chopped basil
90 g (3¼ oz) butter
500 g (1 lb 2 oz/2 cups) ricotta cheese
150 g (5½ oz/1 cup) chopped
  sun-dried capsicum (pepper)
100 g (3½ oz/1 cup) grated parmesan
  cheese
750 ml (26 fl oz/3 cups) Italian
  tomato pasta sauce

Preheat the oven to 180°C (350°F/ Gas 4). Cook the pasta in a large saucepan of rapidly boiling salted water until al dente. Drain well and return to the pan to keep warm. Place the prosciutto, chives and basil in a food processor or blender and pulse until chopped.

Melt the butter in a large frying pan over medium heat. Add the prosciutto mixture and cook for about 5 minutes, or until the prosciutto is golden and crisp. Transfer the mixture to a bowl, add the ricotta cheese, capsicum and a quarter of the parmesan cheese. Stir well and season.

Pour the pasta sauce into a 3 litre (105 fl oz/12 cup) ovenproof dish. Spoon the ricotta mixture into the pasta shells and place in the dish. Sprinkle the remaining parmesan cheese over the shells and bake for 25–30 minutes, or until golden. Spoon the sauce over the shells and serve.

Serves 4–6

## Sweet potato ravioli

500 g (1 lb 2 oz) orange sweet potato,
 chopped
2 teaspoons lemon juice
190 g (6½ oz) butter
50 g (1¾ oz/½ cup) grated
 parmesan cheese
1 tablespoon chopped chives
1 egg, lightly beaten
250 g (9 oz) packet won ton wrappers
2 tablespoons sage, torn
2 tablespoons chopped walnuts

Cook the sweet potato and lemon juice in boiling water for 15 minutes, or until tender. Drain and pat dry with paper towels. Cool for 5 minutes.

Blend the sweet potato and 30 g (1 oz) of the butter in a food processor until smooth. Add the parmesan, chives and half the egg. Season and allow to cool completely.

Put 2 teaspoons of the mixture in the centre of half the won ton wrappers. Brush the edges with the remaining egg, then cover with the remaining wrappers. Press the edges firmly to seal. Using a 7 cm (2¾ inch) cutter, cut the ravioli into circles.

Melt the remaining butter in a small saucepan over low heat and cook until golden brown. Remove from the heat.

Cook the ravioli, in batches, in a large saucepan of boiling water for about 4 minutes. Carefully drain and divide among heated serving plates. Serve the ravioli immediately, drizzled with the butter and scattered with the sage and walnuts.

Serves 4

## Tortellini with eggplant sauce

500 g (1 lb 2 oz) fresh tortellini
3 tablespoons olive oil
2 garlic cloves, crushed
1 red capsicum (pepper), cut into
    squares
500 g (1 lb 2 oz) eggplant (aubergine),
    cut into small cubes
425 g (15 oz) tinned chopped
    tomatoes
250 ml (9 fl oz/1 cup) vegetable stock
2 small handfuls chopped basil

Cook the pasta in a large saucepan of rapidly boiling salted water until al dente. Drain well and return to the pan to keep warm.

Meanwhile, heat the oil in a large saucepan and cook the garlic and capsicum for 1 minute over medium heat. Add the eggplant and stir for 5 minutes or until lightly browned. Add the tomatoes and vegetable stock. Stir to combine and bring to the boil. Reduce the heat to low, cover and cook for 10 minutes or until the vegetables are tender. Add the basil and pasta and toss together.

Serves 4

Hint: Chop the eggplant just before using as it turns brown when exposed to the air.

Long

## Pasta with Gorgonzola sauce

375 g (13 oz) spaghetti or bucatini
200 g (7 oz) Gorgonzola cheese
  (see Note)
250 g (9 oz/1 cup) ricotta cheese
1 tablespoon butter
1 celery stalk, finely chopped
300 ml (10½ fl oz) pouring
  (whipping) cream

Cook the pasta in a large saucepan of rapidly boiling salted water until al dente. Drain well and return to the pan to keep warm. Meanwhile, chop the Gorgonzola into small cubes and beat the ricotta until it is smooth.

Heat the butter in a frying pan over low heat, add the celery and stir for 2 minutes. Add the cream, ricotta and Gorgonzola and season to taste.

Bring to the boil over medium heat, stirring constantly. Reduce the heat and simmer for 1 minute. Toss well with the pasta.

Serves 4–6

Note: Gorgonzola is a rich strong Italian blue-vein cheese.

# Pasta with pesto

500 g (1 lb 2 oz) pasta (see Note)
3 tablespoons pine nuts
2 very large handfuls basil leaves
2 garlic cloves
3 tablespoons grated parmesan
cheese
2 tablespoons grated pecorino cheese
(optional)
125 ml (4 fl oz/½ cup) olive oil

Cook the pasta in a large saucepan of rapidly boiling salted water until al dente. Drain well and return to the pan to keep warm.

Meanwhile, toast the pine nuts in a dry heavy-based frying pan over low heat for 2–3 minutes, or until golden. Allow to cool. Process the pine nuts, basil leaves, garlic, ½ teaspoon of salt and parmesan and pecorino (if using) cheeses in a food processor for 20 seconds, or until finely chopped.

With the motor running, gradually add the oil in a thin steady stream until a paste is formed. Add freshly ground black pepper. Toss the warm pasta in the sauce until well coated.

Serves 4–6

Note: Linguine is traditionally used with pesto but you can serve it with any pasta of your choice. Pesto sauce can be made up to 1 week in advance and refrigerated in an airtight container. Ensure the pesto is tightly packed and seal the surface with some plastic wrap or pour a little oil over the top to prevent the pesto turning black. Each time you use the pesto reseal the surface with a little oil.

# Mediterranean pasta

140 ml (4½ fl oz) olive oil
1 teaspoon dried oregano
5 garlic cloves
6 Roma (plum) tomatoes, halved
500 g (1 lb 2 oz) spaghetti
4 slices prosciutto
16 Kalamata olives
200 g (7 oz) feta cheese,
    cut into bite-sized cubes
1 tablespoon balsamic vinegar
60 g (2¼ oz) rocket (arugula)

Preheat the oven to 150°C (300°F/ Gas 2). Combine 2 tablespoons of the olive oil, oregano, 2 finely chopped garlic cloves and 1 teaspoon salt in a bowl. Add the tomato and toss to combine, rubbing the mixture onto the cut sides. Place the tomato, cut side up, on a lined baking tray and cook in the oven for 1 hour.

Meanwhile, cook the pasta in a large saucepan of rapidly boiling salted water until al dente. Drain well and return to the pan to keep warm. Place the prosciutto on a tray and cook under a hot grill (broiler), turning once, for 3–4 minutes, or until crispy. Break into pieces.

Toss the tomato, olives, feta, spaghetti and balsamic vinegar in a bowl and keep warm.

Thinly slice the remaining garlic cloves. Heat the remaining olive oil in a small saucepan and cook the garlic over low heat, without burning, for 1–2 minutes, or until the garlic has infused the oil.

Pour the garlic and oil over the spaghetti mixture, add the rocket leaves and toss well. Sprinkle with the prosciutto pieces and season well. Serve immediately.

Serves 4

## Bucatini with sausage and fennel seeds

500 g (1 lb 2 oz) Italian sausages
2 tablespoons olive oil
3 garlic cloves, chopped
1 teaspoon fennel seeds
½ teaspoon chilli flakes
850 g (1 lb 14 oz) tinned chopped
  tomatoes
500 g (1 lb 2 oz) bucatini
1 teaspoon balsamic vinegar
1 small handful basil leaves, chopped

Heat a frying pan over high heat, add the sausages and cook, turning regularly, for 8–10 minutes, or until well browned and cooked through. Remove, cool slightly and thinly slice on the diagonal.

Heat the oil in a large saucepan, add the garlic and cook over medium heat for 1 minute. Add the fennel seeds and chilli flakes and cook for a further minute. Stir in the tomato and bring to the boil, then reduce the heat and simmer, covered, for 20 minutes.

Meanwhile, cook the pasta in a large saucepan of rapidly boiling salted water until al dente. Drain well and return to the pan to keep warm.

Add the sausages to the sauce and cook, uncovered, for 5 minutes to heat through. Stir in the balsamic vinegar and basil and toss through the pasta. Divide among bowls, top with the sauce and serve.

Serves 4

## Chilli linguine with chermoula chicken

600 g (1 lb 5 oz) chicken breast fillets
500 g (1 lb 2 oz) chilli linguine

*Chermoula*
2 large handfuls coriander (cilantro)
  leaves, chopped
2 large handfuls flat-leaf (Italian)
  parsley leaves, chopped
4 garlic cloves, crushed
2 teaspoons ground cumin
2 teaspoons ground paprika
125 ml (4 fl oz/1/2 cup) lemon juice
2 teaspoons lemon zest
100 ml (3 1/2 fl oz) olive oil

Heat a large non-stick frying pan over medium heat. Add the chicken breasts and cook until tender. Remove from the pan and leave for 5 minutes before cutting into thin slices.

Cook the pasta in a large saucepan of rapidly boiling salted water until al dente. Drain well and return to the pan to keep warm.

Meanwhile, combine the chermoula ingredients in a glass bowl and add the sliced chicken. Leave to stand until the pasta has finished cooking. Serve the pasta topped with the chermoula chicken.

Serves 4

## Pastitsio

2 tablespoons oil
4 garlic cloves, crushed
2 onions, chopped
1 kg (2 lb 4 oz) minced (ground) beef
1 kg (2 lb 4 oz) tinned chopped
  tomatoes
250 ml (9 fl oz/1 cup) dry red whine
250 ml (9 fl oz/1 cup) beef stock
1 bay leaf
1 teaspoon dried mixed herbs
350 g (12 oz) ziti (see Note)
3 eggs, lightly beaten
500 g (1 lb 2 oz/2 cups) Greek-style
  yoghurt
200 g (7 oz) kefalotyri cheese, grated
½ teaspoon ground nutmeg
60 g (2¼ oz/½ cup) grated cheddar
  cheese
oakleaf lettuce, for serving

Heat the oil in a large heavy-based saucepan, and cook the garlic and onion over medium heat for 5 minutes, or until the onion is soft. Add the beef and cook over high heat, until browned, then drain off any excess fat. Add the tomato, wine, stock, bay leaf and herbs and bring to the boil. Reduce the heat and simmer for 40 minutes. Season well.

Preheat the oven to 180°C (350°F/ Gas 4). Cook the pasta in a large saucepan of rapidly boiling salted water, until al dente. Drain well and spread in the base of a large ovenproof dish. Pour in half the egg and top with the sauce. Combine the yoghurt, remaining egg, kefalotyri and nutmeg and pour over the top. Sprinkle with the cheddar and bake for 40 minutes, or until lightly golden brown. Leave to stand for 10 minutes before serving with oakleaf lettuce.

Serves 6-8

Note: Ziti is a wide tubular pasta. You could use fettuccine or spaghetti.

## Tagliatelle with salmon and creamy dill dressing

350 g (12 oz) fresh tagliatelle
3 tablespoons olive oil
3 x 200 g (7 oz) salmon fillets, skinned
  and boned (ask your fishmonger
  to do this)
3 garlic cloves, crushed
375 ml (13 fl oz/1½ cups) pouring
  (whipping) cream
1½ tablespoons chopped dill
1 teaspoon mustard powder
1 tablespoon lemon juice

Cook the pasta in a large saucepan of rapidly boiling salted water until al dente. Drain well, toss with 1 tablespoon of the oil and return to the pan to keep warm.

Meanwhile, heat the remaining oil in a large deep frying pan and cook the salmon for 2 minutes each side, or until crisp on the outside but still pink on the inside. Remove from the pan, cut into small cubes and keep warm.

In the same pan, cook the garlic for 30 seconds, or until fragrant. Add the cream, dill and mustard powder, bring to the boil, then reduce the heat and simmer, stirring, for 4–5 minutes, or until thickened. Season.

Add the salmon and any juices plus the lemon juice to the creamy dill sauce and stir until warmed through. Gently toss the sauce and salmon through the pasta and divide among serving bowls.

Serves 4

# Spaghetti Niçoise

350 g (12 oz) spaghetti
8 quail eggs (or 4 hen eggs)
1 lemon
550 g (1 lb 4 oz) tinned tuna in oil
60 g (2¼ oz) pitted and halved
Kalamata olives
100 g (3½ oz) semi-dried (sun-
blushed) tomatoes, halved
lengthways
4 anchovy fillets, chopped into small
pieces
3 tablespoons baby capers in brine,
drained, rinsed and patted dry
3 tablespoons chopped flat-leaf
(Italian) parsley

Cook the pasta in a large saucepan
of rapidly boiling salted water until
al dente. Drain well and return to the
pan to keep warm.

Meanwhile, place the eggs in a
saucepan of cold water, bring to
the boil and cook for 4 minutes
(10 minutes for hen eggs). Drain, cool
under cold water, then peel. Cut the
eggs in half (or the hen eggs into
quarters). Finely grate the zest of the
lemon to give 1 teaspoon of grated
zest, then squeeze the lemon to give
2 tablespoons juice.

Empty the tuna and its oil into a large
bowl. Add the olives, tomato halves,
anchovy, lemon zest and juice, capers
and 2 tablespoons of the parsley.
Toss the pasta gently through the
tuna mixture. Garnish with the egg
and the remaining parsley to serve.

Serves 4–6

## Spaghetti vongole

375 g (13 oz) spaghetti
125 ml (4 fl oz/½ cup) extra virgin
  olive oil
40 g (1½ oz) butter
1 small onion, very finely chopped
6 large garlic cloves, finely chopped
125 ml (4 fl oz/½ cup) dry white wine
1 kg (2 lb 4 oz) clams (vongole),
  soaked in cold water for 30 minutes,
  then drained
1 small red chilli, seeded and finely
  chopped
1 handful flat-leaf (Italian) parsley
  leaves, chopped

Cook the pasta in a large saucepan of rapidly boiling salted water until al dente. Drain well and return to the pan to keep warm.

Heat the oil and 1 tablespoon of the butter in a large saucepan over medium heat. Add the onion and half the garlic and cook for 10 minutes, or until lightly golden—ensure the garlic doesn't start to burn. Add the wine and cook for 2 minutes. Then add the clams, chilli and remaining butter and garlic and cook, covered, for 8 minutes, shaking regularly, until the clams pop open—discard any that are still closed.

Stir in the parsley and season.
Add the hot pasta and toss well.

Serves 4

# Pasta alla Norma

185 ml (6 fl oz/³⁄₄ cup) olive oil
1 onion, finely chopped
2 garlic cloves, finely chopped
2 x 400 g (14 oz) tins chopped
tomatoes
400 g (14 oz) bucatini or spaghetti
1 large eggplant (aubergine), about
500 g (1 lb 2 oz)
1 handufl basil leaves, torn,
plus extra for garnishing
60 g (½ cup) ricotta salata (see Note),
crumbled
45 g (1½ oz/½ cup) grated pecorino
or parmesan cheese
1 tablespoon extra virgin olive oil,
to drizzle

Heat 2 tablespoons of the olive oil in a frying pan and cook the onion over medium heat for 5 minutes, or until softened. Stir in the garlic and cook for 30 seconds. Add the tomato and season. Reduce the heat to low and cook for 20–25 minutes, or until the sauce has thickened and reduced.

Meanwhile, cook the pasta in a saucepan of rapidly boiling salted water until al dente. Drain well and return to the pan to keep warm.

Cut the eggplant lengthways into 5 mm (¼ inch) thick slices. Heat the remaining olive oil in a large frying pan. When the oil is hot but not smoking, add the eggplant slices, a few at a time, and cook for 3–5 minutes, or until lightly browned. Drain on paper towels. Add the eggplant to the sauce with the basil, stirring over low heat.

Add the hot pasta to the sauce with half each of the ricotta and pecorino and toss together well. Serve immediately, sprinkled with the remaining cheeses and extra basil and drizzled with extra virgin olive oil.

Serves 4–6

Note: Ricotta salata is a lightly salted, pressed ricotta cheese. If unavailable, use a mild feta cheese.

## Buckwheat pasta with cabbage, potato and cheese sauce

350 g (12 oz) Savoy cabbage,
   roughly chopped
175 g (6 oz) potatoes, cut into 2 cm
   (3/4 inch) cubes
500 g (1 lb 2 oz) buckwheat pasta
   (see Note)
80 ml (2½ fl oz/⅓ cup) extra virgin
   olive oil
1 small bunch sage, finely chopped
2 garlic cloves, finely chopped
350 g (12 oz) mixed cheeses,
   such as mascarpone, fontina,
   Taleggio and Gorgonzola
grated parmesan cheese, for serving

Bring a large saucepan of salted water to the boil. Add the cabbage, potato and pasta and cook for 3–5 minutes, or until the pasta and vegetables are cooked through. Drain, reserving 250 ml (9 fl oz/1 cup) of the cooking water.

Dry the saucepan, then add the oil and gently cook the sage and garlic for 1 minute. Add the mixed cheeses to the pan. Mix briefly, and add the pasta, cabbage and potatoes. Season and remove from the heat and gently stir the mixture together, adding some of the reserved pasta water to loosen it up a little, if necessary. Serve with parmesan sprinkled over the top.

Serves 6

Note: Buckwheat pasta is called pizzoccheri in Italy. This type of pasta is popular in Valtellina, near the Swiss border, and is traditionally served with potatoes, cabbage and cheese.

## Pasta with creamy tomato and bacon sauce

400 g (14 oz) bucatini
1 tablespoon olive oil
180 g (6¼ oz) streaky bacon, thinly
   sliced (see Note)
500 g (1 lb 2 oz) Roma (plum)
   tomatoes, roughly chopped
125 ml (4 fl oz/½ cup) thickened
   (whipping) cream
2 tablespoons sun-dried tomato pesto
2 tablespoons finely chopped flat-leaf
   (Italian) parsley
50 g (1¾ oz/½ cup) grated
   parmesan cheese

Cook the pasta in a large saucepan of rapidly boiling salted water until al dente. Drain well and return to the pan to keep warm.

Meanwhile, heat the oil in a frying pan, add the bacon and cook over high heat for 2 minutes, or until starting to brown. Reduce the heat to medium, add the tomato and cook, stirring frequently, for 2 minutes, or until the tomato has softened but still holds its shape.

Add the cream and tomato pesto and stir until heated through. Remove from the heat, add the parsley, then toss the sauce through the pasta with the grated parmesan cheese.

Serves 4

Note: Streaky bacon is the tail fatty ends of bacon rashers and adds flavour to the dish. You can use ordinary slices bacon, if you prefer.

# Ziti with sausage

1 red capsicum (pepper)
1 green capsicum (pepper)
1 small eggplant (aubergine), sliced
3 tablespoons olive oil
1 onion, sliced
1 garlic clove, crushed
250 g (9 oz) chipolata sausages,
  sliced
425 g (15 oz) tinned chopped
  tomatoes
125 ml (4 fl oz/½ cup) red wine
3 tablespoons pitted black olives,
  halved
1 tablespoon chopped basil
1 tablespoon chopped flat-leaf
  (Italian) parsley
500 g (1 lb 2 oz) ziti (see Note)

Cut both capsicum into large flat pieces, removing the seeds and membranes. Place, skin side up, under a hot grill (broiler) until the skin blackens and blisters. Cool in a plastic bag, then peel off the skin. Chop and set aside.

Brush the eggplant with a little oil. Grill (broil) until golden on each side, brushing with more oil as required. Set aside.

Heat the remaining oil in a frying pan. Add the onion and garlic and stir over low heat until the onion is tender. Add the chipolatas and cook until well browned.

Stir in the tomato, wine, olives, basil and parsley and season. Bring to the boil. Reduce the heat and simmer for 15 minutes. Add the vegetables and heat through.

Meanwhile, cook the ziti in a large saucepan of rapidly boiling salted water until al dente. Drain well and return to the pan to keep warm. Toss the vegetables and sauce through the pasta.

serves 4

Note: Ziti is a wide tubular pasta. You could use fettuccine or spaghetti.

# Tagliatelle with chicken livers and cream

2 tablespoons olive oil
1 onion, finely chopped
1 garlic clove, crushed
300 g (10½ oz) chicken livers,
    chopped into small pieces
250 ml (9 fl oz/1 cup) pouring
    (whipping) cream
1 tablespoon snipped chives
1 teaspoon wholegrain mustard
2 eggs, lightly beaten
375 g (13 oz) tagliatelle

Heat the oil in a large frying pan. Add the onion and garlic and stir over low heat until the onion is tender. Add the chicken livers to the pan and cook gently for 2–3 minutes. Remove from the heat.

Stir in the cream, chives and mustard and season. Return to the heat and bring the sauce to the boil. Add the eggs, stirring gently. Remove from the heat.

Meanwhile, cook the pasta in a large saucepan of rapidly boiling salted water until al dente. Drain well and return to the pan to keep warm. Add the sauce and toss well to combine. Serve in warmed pasta bowls.

Serves 4

## Spaghetti with anchovies, capers and chilli

400 g (14 oz) spaghettini
125 ml (4 fl oz/½ cup) olive oil
4 garlic cloves, finely chopped
10 anchovies, chopped
1 tablespoon salted baby capers, rinsed and patted dry
1 teaspoon chilli flakes
2 tablespoons lemon juice
2 teaspoons finely grated lemon zest
3 tablespoons chopped flat-leaf (Italian) parsley
3 tablespoons chopped basil
3 tablespoons chopped mint
50 g (1¾ oz/½ cup) shredded parmesan cheese, plus extra for serving
extra virgin olive oil, to drizzle

Cook the pasta in a saucepan of boiling salted water until al dente.

Heat the olive oil in a frying pan and cook the garlic over medium heat for 2–3 minutes, or until starting to brown. Add the anchovies, capers and chilli and cook for 1 minute.

Add the hot pasta to the pan with the lemon juice, zest, parsley, basil, mint and parmesan. Season and toss together well.

To serve, drizzle with a extra virgin olive oil and sprinkle with parmesan.

Serves 4

## Creamy tomato and prawn pasta

400 g (14 oz) dried egg tagliatelle
1 tablespoon olive oil
3 garlic cloves, finely chopped
20 medium raw prawns (shrimp),
   peeled and deveined with tails intact
550 g (1 lb 4 oz) Roma (plum)
   tomatoes, diced
2 tablespoons thinly sliced basil,
   plus whole leaves for garnishing
125 ml (4 fl oz/½ cup) white wine
80 ml (2½ fl oz/⅓ cup) pouring
   (whipping) cream

Cook the pasta in a large saucepan of boiling salted water until al dente. Drain and keep warm, reserving 2 tablespoons of the cooking water.

Meanwhile, heat the oil and garlic in a large frying pan over low heat for 1–2 minutes. Increase the heat to medium, add the prawns and cook for 3–5 minutes, stirring frequently until cooked. Remove the prawns and keep warm.

Add the tomato and sliced basil and stir for 3 minutes, or until the tomato is soft. Pour in the wine and cream, bring to the boil and simmer for 2 minutes.

Purée the sauce in a blender, return to the pan, then add the reserved pasta water and bring to a simmer. Stir in the prawns until heated through. Toss through the pasta and serve garnished with the basil leaves.

Serves 4

## Pasta with roasted chicken, pine nuts and lemon

1.3 kg (3 lb) chicken
1 garlic bulb, cloves separated
  and unpeeled
3 tablespoons olive oil
30 g (1 oz) butter, softened
1 tablespoon finely chopped thyme
125 ml (4 fl oz/½ cup) lemon juice
500 g (1 lb 2 oz) bavette or spaghetti
2 tablespoons currants
1 teaspoon finely grated lemon zest
50 g (1¾ oz/⅓ cup) pine nuts, toasted
1 handful flat-leaf (Italian) parsley
  leaves, finely chopped

Preheat the oven to 200°C (400°F/ Gas 6). Remove the neck from the inside of the chicken and place the neck in a roasting tin. Rinse the inside of the chicken with cold water and pat dry. Insert the garlic cloves into the cavity, then put the chicken in the tin.

Combine the oil, butter, thyme and lemon juice, then rub over the chicken and season. Roast for 1 hour, or until golden and the juices run clear when the thigh is pierced with a skewer. Transfer the chicken to a bowl to catch any juices while resting. Remove the garlic from the cavity, cool, then squeeze the garlic out of their skins and finely chop.

Cook the pasta in a large saucepan of rapidly boiling salted water until al dente. Drain well and return to the pan to keep warm.

Meanwhile, pour the juices from the roasting tin into a saucepan and discard the neck. Add the currants, zest and chopped garlic, then simmer over low heat.

Remove the meat from the chicken and shred. Add the resting juices to the pan. Add the chicken, pine nuts, parsley and the sauce to the hot pasta and toss well. Season and serve.

Serves 4–6

## Spaghetti with shellfish and white wine sauce

500 g (1 lb 2 oz) mussels
1 kg (2 lb 4 oz) clams (vongole)
400 g (14 oz) spaghetti
2 tablespoons olive oil
4 French shallots (eschalots),
    finely chopped
2 garlic cloves, crushed
250 ml (9 fl oz/1 cup) dry white wine
3 tablespoons chopped flat-leaf
    (Italian) parsley

Scrub the mussels with a stiff brush and remove any barnacles with a knife. Pull away the hairy beards. Discard any mussels or clams that are broken or open ones that do not close when tapped on a work surface. Wash them thoroughly under cold running water.

Cook the pasta in a large saucepan of rapidly boiling salted water until al dente. Drain well and return to the pan to keep warm.

Meanwhile, heat the oil in a large saucepan over medium heat and cook the shallots for 4 minutes, or until softened. Add the garlic and cook for a further 1 minute. Pour in the wine, bring to the boil and cook for 2 minutes, or until reduced slightly. Add the clams and mussels, tossing to coat them in the liquid, then cover the pan. Cook, shaking the pan regularly, for about 3 minutes, or until the shells have opened. Discard any clams or mussels that do not open. Toss the clam mixture through the spaghetti, scatter with parsley and transfer to a warmed serving dish. Season and serve.

Serves 4

## Low-fat linguine with bacon, mushrooms and peas

3 slices bacon
2 teaspoons olive oil
2–3 garlic cloves, crushed
1 red onion, chopped
185 g (6½ oz) field mushrooms, sliced
1 very large handful chopped flat-leaf
  (Italian) parsley leaves
150 g (5½ oz/1 cup) peas
375 ml (13 fl oz/1½ cups) light
  evaporated milk
2 teaspoons cornflour (cornstarch)
325 g (11½ oz) linguine

Remove the fat from the bacon and chop roughly. Heat the oil in a saucepan, add the garlic, onion and bacon and cook over low heat for 5 minutes, stirring frequently, until the onion and bacon are soft. Add the sliced mushrooms and cook, stirring, for another 5 minutes, or until soft.

Add the parsley, peas and milk to the pan. Mix the cornflour with 1 tablespoon water until smooth, add to the mixture and stir over medium heat until slightly thickened.

Cook the pasta in a large saucepan of rapidly boiling salted water until al dente. Drain well and serve with the hot sauce and parmesan shavings.

Serves 4

Note: Parmesan cheese adds a nice flavour to this dish, but leave it out if you are wanting a meal with a very low-fat content.

## Pasta with beef ragù

100 g streaky bacon or pancetta,
   finely chopped
1 onion, finely chopped
3 garlic cloves, crushed
1 bay leaf
800 g (1 lb 12 oz) lean minced
   (ground) beef
500 ml (17 fl oz/2 cups) red wine
90 g (3¼ oz/⅓ cup) tomato paste
   (concentrated purée)
400 g (14 oz) tagliatelle
grated parmesan cheese, for serving

Heat a large deep frying pan (preferably stainless steel or non-coated). Add the bacon or pancetta and cook over medium–high heat for 2 minutes, or until soft and just starting to brown. Add the onion, garlic and bay leaf and cook for 2 minutes, or until the onion is soft and just starting to brown.

Add the beef and stir for about 4 minutes, or until the beef browns, breaking up any lumps with the back of a wooden spoon. Add the wine, tomato paste and 250 ml (9 fl oz/1 cup) water and stir well. Bring to the boil, then reduce the heat and simmer, covered, for 40 minutes. Remove the lid and cook for another 40 minutes, or until reduced to a thick, glossy sauce.

About 20 minutes before the ragù is ready, cook the pasta in a large saucepan of rapidly boiling salted water until al dente. Drain well. Serve the sauce over the pasta and garnish with a little grated parmesan.

Serves 4

# Spaghettini with squid in black ink

1 kg (2 lb 4 oz) whole squid
2 tablespoons olive oil
1 onion, finely chopped
6 garlic cloves, finely chopped
1 bay leaf
1 small red chilli, seeded
    and thinly sliced
80 ml (2½ fl oz/⅓ cup) white wine
80 ml (2½ fl oz/⅓ cup) dry vermouth
250 ml (9 fl oz/1 cup) fish stock
3 tablespoons tomato paste
    (concentrated purée)
500 ml (17 fl oz/2 cups) Italian
    tomato pasta sauce
15 g (½ oz) squid ink
500 g (1 lb 2 oz) spaghettini
½ teaspoon Pernod (optional)
1 small handufl flat-leaf (Italian) parsley
    leaves, chopped
1 garlic clove, extra, crushed

To clean the squid, pull the tentacles away from the hood (the intestines should come away at the same time). Remove the intestines by cutting under the eyes, and remove the beak. Pull out the transparent quill from inside the body. Remove any white membrane. Thinly slice the squid and the tentacles.

Heat the oil in a saucepan over medium heat. Add the onion and cook until lightly golden. Add the garlic, bay leaf and chilli and cook for 2 minutes, or until the garlic is lightly golden. Stir in the wine, vermouth, stock, tomato paste and sauce and 250 ml (9 fl oz/ 1 cup) of water, then bring to the boil. Reduce to a simmer and cook for 45 minutes, or until the liquid has reduced by half. Add the squid ink and cook for 2 minutes, or until the sauce is evenly black and glossy.

Meanwhile, cook the pasta in a large saucepan of rapidly boiling salted water until al dente. Drain well and return to the pan to keep warm.

Add the squid and Pernod, stir well, then cook for 4–5 minutes, or until it turns opaque and is cooked through. Stir in the parsley and the extra garlic and season. Toss through the hot pasta and serve immediately.

Serves 4–6

## Spaghetti with meatballs

500 g (1 lb 2 oz) spaghetti

*Meatballs*
500 g (1 lb 2 oz) minced (ground) beef
40 g (1½ oz/½ cup) fresh
   breadcrumbs
1 onion, finely chopped
2 garlic cloves, crushed
2 teaspoons Worcestershire sauce
1 teaspoon dried oregano
3 tablespoons plain (all-purpose) flour
2 tablespoons olive oil

*Sauce*
2 x 400 g (14 oz) tins chopped
   tomatoes
1 tablespoon olive oil
1 onion, finely chopped
2 garlic cloves, crushed
2 tablespoons tomato paste
   (concentrated purée)

To make the meatballs, combine the beef, breadcrumbs, onion, garlic, Worcestershire sauce and oregano in a bowl and season. Use your hands to mix the ingredients together well. Roll level tablespoons of the mixture into balls, dust lightly with flour and shake off the excess. Heat the oil in a deep frying pan and cook the meatballs, in batches, turning frequently, until browned all over. Drain well.

To make the sauce, purée the tomatoes in a food processor or blender. Heat the oil in a clean pan. Add the onion and cook over medium heat for a few minutes until soft and lightly golden. Add the garlic and cook for another minute. Add the puréed tomatoes, paste, stock and sugar to the pan and stir to combine. Bring the mixture to the boil and add the meatballs. Reduce the heat and simmer for 15 minutes, turning the meatballs once. Season.

Meanwhile, cook the spaghetti in a large saucepan of rapidly boiling salted water until al dente. Drain and divide among serving bowls, top with the meatballs and sauce.

Serves 4

## Fettuccine with creamy spinach and roasted tomato

6 Roma (plum) tomatoes
40 g (1½ oz) butter
2 garlic cloves, crushed
1 onion, chopped
500 g (1 lb 2 oz) English spinach,
  trimmed
250 ml (9 fl oz/1 cup) vegetable stock
125 ml (4 fl oz/½ cup) thick
  (double/heavy) cream
500 g (1 lb 2 oz) fresh spinach
  fettuccine
50 g (1¾ oz) shaved parmesan
  cheese

Preheat the oven to 220°C (425°F/ Gas 7). Cut the tomatoes in half lengthways, then cut each half into three wedges. Place the wedges on a lightly greased baking tray and bake for 30–35 minutes, or until softened and slightly golden.

Meanwhile, heat the butter in a large frying pan. Add the garlic and onion and cook over medium heat for 5 minutes, or until the onion is soft. Add the spinach, stock and cream, increase the heat to high and bring to the boil. Simmer rapidly for 5 minutes.

While the spinach mixture is cooking, cook the pasta in a large saucepan of boiling water until al dente. Drain and return to the pan. Remove the spinach mixture from the heat and season well. Cool slightly, then process in a food processor until smooth. Toss through the pasta until well coated. Divide among serving bowls, top with the roasted tomatoes and parmesan shavings and serve.

Serves 4–6

## Summer seafood marinara

300 g (10½ oz) fresh saffron
  angel hair pasta
1 tablespoon extra virgin olive oil
30 g (1 oz) butter
2 garlic cloves, finely chopped
1 large onion, finely chopped
1 small red chilli, finely chopped
600 g (1 lb 5 oz) tinned chopped
  tomatoes
250 ml (9 fl oz/1 cup) white wine
finely grated zest of 1 lemon
½ teaspoon white sugar
200 g (7 oz) scallops without roe
500 g (1 lb 2 oz) raw prawns (shrimp),
  peeled and deveined
300 g (10 ½ oz) clams (vongole),
  soaked in cold water for 30 minutes,
  then drained

Cook the pasta in a large saucepan
of rapidly boiling salted water, until
al dente. Drain and keep warm.

Heat the oil and butter in a large frying
pan, add the garlic, onion and chilli
and cook over medium heat for
5 minutes, or until soft but not golden.
Add the tomatoes and wine and bring
to the boil. Cook for 10 minutes,
or until the sauce has reduced and
thickened slightly.

Add the lemon zest, sugar, scallops,
prawns and clams and cook, covered,
for 5 minutes or until the seafood is
tender. Discard any clams that do not
open. Season and serve the sauce on
top of the pasta.

Serves 4

# Farmhouse pasta

375 g (13 oz) ziti (see Note)
1 large all-purpose potato,
cut into small cubes
400 g (14 oz) broccoli
80 ml (2½ fl oz/⅓ cup) olive oil
3 garlic cloves, crushed
1 small red chilli, finely chopped
800 g (1 lb 12 oz) tinned chopped
tomatoes
30 g (1 oz/⅓ cup) shredded pecorino
cheese

Bring a large saucepan of salted water
to the boil and cook the pasta and
potato together for 8–10 minutes, or
until the pasta is al dente. Drain and
return to the pan.

Meanwhile, trim the broccoli into
florets and discard the stems. Place
in a saucepan of boiling water and
cook for 1–2 minutes, then drain and
plunge into iced water. Drain and add
to the cooked pasta and potato.

Heat the oil in a saucepan, add
the garlic and chilli and cook for
30 seconds. Add the tomato and
simmer for 5 minutes, or until slightly
reduced and thickened. Season.

Pour the tomato mixture over the
pasta, potato and broccoli. Toss well
and stir over low heat until warmed
through. Serve sprinkled with cheese.

Serves 4

Note: Ziti is a wide tubular pasta.
You could use fettuccine or spaghetti.

## Pasta with rocket and mushrooms

15 g (½ oz) dried porcini mushrooms
375 g (13 oz) fettuccine
20 g (¾ oz) butter
3 tablespoons extra virgin olive oil
2 garlic cloves, crushed
250 g (9 oz) button mushrooms, sliced
3 tablespoons lemon juice
30 g (1 oz) grated parmesan cheese
90 g (3¼ oz) baby rocket (arugula)

Soak the porcini mushrooms in 80 ml (2½ fl oz/⅓ cup) of boiling water for 10 minutes to soften. Cook the pasta in a large saucepan of rapidly boiling salted water until al dente. Drain well and return to the pan to keep warm.

Meanwhile, heat the butter and oil over medium heat in a frying pan. Add the garlic and button mushrooms and cook for 4 minutes, tossing occasionally. Drain the porcini mushrooms, reserving the soaking liquid. Chop all of the mushrooms, then add them to the frying pan with the soaking liquid. Bring to a simmer.

Add the mushroom mixture, lemon juice and parmesan to the pan with the pasta and toss together. Season and toss through the rocket just before serving.

Serves 4

## Spaghetti with herbs, baby spinach and garlic crumbs

375 g (13 oz) spaghetti
125 g (4½ oz) day-old crusty Italian
  bread, crusts removed
100 ml (3½ fl oz) extra virgin olive oil,
  plus extra for serving
4 garlic cloves, finely chopped
400 g (14 oz) baby spinach leaves
1 handful basil leaves, chopped
1 large handful flat-leaf (Italian) parsley
  leaves, chopped
1 tablespoon thyme leaves

Cook the pasta in a large saucepan of rapidly boiling salted water until al dente. Drain well and return to the pan to keep warm, reserving 125 ml (4 fl oz/½ cup) of the cooking water.

To make the garlic breadcrumbs, mix the bread in a food processor or blender until coarse crumbs form. Heat 1 tablespoon of oil in a saucepan. Add the breadcrumbs and half the garlic and toss for 2–3 minutes, or until lightly golden. Remove and clean the pan with paper towels.

Heat 2 tablespoons of the oil in the same pan. Add the spinach and remaining garlic, toss together for 1 minute, then add the herbs. Cook, tossing frequently, for a further 1 minute to wilt the herbs a little and to heat through. Toss through the pasta with the remaining oil and reserved pasta water. Divide among serving bowls and scatter with the garlic breadcrumbs. Serve drizzled with extra virgin olive oil.

Serves 4

## Paprika veal with caraway noodles

3 tablespoons olive oil
1 kg (2 lb 4 oz) diced veal shoulder
1 large onion, thinly sliced
3 garlic cloves, finely chopped
3 tablespoons Hungarian paprika
1/2 teaspoon caraway seeds
2 x 400 g (14 oz) tins chopped
   tomatoes, one drained
350 g (12 oz) fresh fettuccine
40 g (1½ oz) butter, softened

Heat half the oil in a large saucepan over medium–high heat, then brown the veal, in batches, for 3 minutes per batch. Remove the veal from the pan and set aside with any pan juices.

Add the remaining oil to the pan and sauté the onion and garlic over medium heat for 5 minutes, or until softened. Add the paprika and 1/4 teaspoon of the caraway seeds and stir for 30 seconds.

Add the chopped tomatoes and their liquid plus 125 ml (4 fl oz/½ cup) water. Return the veal to the pan with any juices, increase the heat to high and bring to the boil. Reduce the heat to low, then cover and simmer for 1 hour 15 minutes, or until the meat is tender and the sauce has thickened.

About 15 minutes before the veal is ready, cook the pasta in a large saucepan of rapidly boiling salted water until al dente. Drain, then return to the pan. Stir in the butter and the remaining caraway seeds. Serve immediately with the veal.

Serves 4

## Spaghetti Bolognese

60 g (2¼ oz) butter
1 onion, finely chopped
2 garlic cloves, crushed
1 celery stalk, finely chopped
1 carrot, diced
50 g (1¾ oz) piece pancetta, diced
500 g (1 lb 2 oz) minced (ground) beef
1 tablespoon chopped oregano
250 ml (9 fl oz/1 cup) red wine
500 ml (17 fl oz/2 cups) beef stock
2 tablespoons tomato paste
  (concentrated purée)
2 x 400 g (14 oz) tins crushed
  tomatoes
400 g (14 oz) spaghetti
3 tablespoons grated parmesan
  cheese

Melt the butter in a large saucepan, add the onion and cook over medium heat for 2–3 minutes, or until it starts to soften. Add the garlic, celery and carrot, and cook, stirring, over low heat, for 5 minutes. Increase the heat to high, add the pancetta, beef and oregano, and cook for 4–5 minutes, or until browned. Use a fork to break up any lumps.

Pour in the wine, reduce the heat and simmer for 4–5 minutes, or until it is absorbed. Add the stock, tomato paste and tomato and season well. Cover with a lid and simmer for 1½ hours, stirring occasionally to prevent the sauce from catching on the bottom of the saucepan. Uncover and simmer for another hour, stirring occasionally.

Cook the spaghetti in a large saucepan of rapidly boiling salted water until al dente. Drain well, divide among serving plates and top with the sauce. Sprinkle with the parmesan and serve.

Serves 4

## Tagliatelle with octopus

500 g (1 lb 2 oz) tagliatelle
2 tablespoons olive oil
1 onion, sliced
1 garlic clove, crushed
425 g (15 oz) tinned chopped
  tomatoes
125 ml (4 fl oz/½ cup) dry white wine
1 tablespoon chilli sauce
1 tablespoon chopped basil
1 kg (2 lb 4 oz) baby octopus, cleaned
  and halved (see Note)

Cook the pasta in a large saucepan of rapidly boiling salted water until al dente. Drain well and return to the pan to keep warm.

Meanwhile, heat the oil in a large frying pan. Add the onion and garlic and stir over low heat until the onion is tender. Add the tomato, wine, chilli sauce, basil and season. Bring to the boil. Reduce the heat and simmer for 10 minutes.

Add the octopus to the sauce. Simmer for 5–10 minutes or until the octopus is tender. Pour over the pasta and serve immediately.

Serves 4

Note: To clean octopus, use a small sharp knife and remove the gut by either cutting off the head entirely or by slicing open the head and removing the gut. Pick up the body and use your index finger to push the beak up. Remove the beak. Wash the octopus thoroughly. Cut the sac into two or three pieces.

## Pasta and spinach timbales

30 g (1 oz) butter
1 tablespoon olive oil
1 onion, chopped
500 g (1 lb 2 oz) English spinach
 leaves, blanched and drained well
8 eggs, lightly beaten
250 ml (9 fl oz/1 cup) pouring
 (whipping) cream
100 g (3½ oz) spaghetti, cooked
60 g (2¼ oz/½ cup) grated
 cheddar cheese
60 g (2¼ oz) grated parmesan cheese

Preheat the oven to 180°C (350°F/
Gas 4). Brush six 250 ml (9 fl oz/
1 cup) ramekins with melted butter or
oil. Line the bases with baking paper.
Heat the butter and oil together in
a frying pan. Add the onion and stir
over low heat until tender. Add the
spinach and cook for 1 minute.
Remove from the heat and allow to
cool. Whisk in the eggs and cream.
Stir in the spaghetti, cheeses, season
and stir well. Spoon into the ramekins.

Place the ramekins in a roasting tin.
Pour boiling water into the tin to come
halfway up the sides of the ramekins.
Bake for 30–35 minutes, or until set.
Halfway through cooking, you may
need to cover with a sheet of foil to
prevent overbrowning. Near the end
of cooking time, test the timbales with
the point of a knife—the knife should
come out clean.

Allow the timbales to rest for
15 minutes, then run the point of a
knife around the edge of each ramekin
and turn out onto serving plates.

Serves 6

## Bucatini with eggplant and mushrooms

2 tablespoons olive oil
250 g (9 oz) mushrooms, sliced
1 eggplant (aubergine), diced
2 garlic cloves, crushed
820 g (1 lb 13 oz) tinned chopped
  tomatoes
500 g (1 lb 2 oz) bucatini or spaghetti
1 large handful chopped flat-leaf
  (Italian) parsley leaves (optional)

Heat the oil in a frying pan and cook the mushrooms, eggplant and garlic, stirring, for 4 minutes. Add the tomato, cover and simmer for 15 minutes.

Meanwhile, cook the pasta in a large saucepan of rapidly boiling salted water until al dente. Drain well and return to the pan to keep warm.

Season the sauce and stir in the parsley. Toss with the pasta and serve.

Serves 4–6

## Ziti carbonara

500 g (1 lb 2 oz) ziti (see Note)
1 tablespoon olive oil
200 g (7 oz) pancetta, cut into
  long thin strips
4 egg yolks
300 ml (10½ fl oz) pouring
  (whipping) cream
50 g (1¾ oz/½ cup) grated
  parmesan cheese
2 tablespoons finely chopped flat-leaf
  (Italian) parsley

Cook the pasta in a large saucepan of rapidly boiling salted water until al dente. Drain well and return to the pan to keep warm.

Meanwhile, heat the olive oil in a non-stick frying pan and cook the pancetta over high heat for 6 minutes, or until crisp and golden.

Beat the egg yolks, cream and parmesan together in a bowl and season generously. Pour over the hot pasta in the saucepan and toss gently. Add the pancetta and parsley. Return the pan to very low heat and cook for 30–60 seconds, or until the sauce has thickened and coats the pasta. Don't cook over high heat or the eggs will scramble. Season and serve with extra parmesan, if desired.

Serves 4–6

Note: Ziti is a wide tubular pasta. You could use fettuccine or spaghetti.

## Salami pasta salad

1 red capsicum (pepper),
  cut into strips
1 green capsicum (pepper),
  cut into strips
4 celery stalks, sliced
1 fennel bulb, trimmed and sliced
1 red onion, sliced
200 g (7 oz) salami, thickly sliced
  and then cut into strips
1 large handful flat-leaf (Italian) parsley
  leaves, chopped
300 g (10½ oz) fettuccine

*Dressing*
125 ml (4 fl oz/½ cup) olive oil
3 tablespoons lemon juice
2½ tablespoons Dijon mustard
1 teaspoon white sugar
1 garlic clove, crushed

Mix together the capsicum, celery, fennel, onion, salami and parsley in a large bowl.

Cook the pasta in a large saucepan of rapidly boiling salted water until al dente. Drain well and rinse under cold water. Add to the bowl and toss with the vegetables and salami.

To make the dressing, combine the olive oil, lemon juice, mustard, sugar and crushed garlic and season. Pour over the pasta salad and toss well.

Serves 8

## Fettuccine with cherry tomatoes, avocado and bacon

4 garlic cloves, unpeeled
80 ml (2½ fl oz/⅓ cup) olive oil
250 g (9 oz) cherry tomatoes
300 g (10½ oz) short-cut bacon
  (see Note)
350 g (11 oz) fresh fettuccine
1 tablespoon white wine vinegar
2 tablespoons chopped basil,
  plus whole leaves for garnishing
2 ripe avocados, diced

Preheat the oven to 200°C (400°F/ Gas 6). Place the garlic at one end of a roasting tin and drizzle with 2 tablespoons of the olive oil. Place the tomatoes at the other end and season well. Bake for 10 minutes, then remove the garlic. Return the tomatoes to the oven for a further 5–10 minutes, or until soft.

Cook the bacon under a hot grill (broiler) for 4–5 minutes each side, or until crisp and golden. Roughly chop.

Meanwhile, cook the pasta in a large pan of rapidly boiling salted water until al dente. Drain well and transfer to a large bowl. Drizzle 1 tablespoon of the olive oil over the pasta and toss well. Season and keep warm.

Slit the skin of each garlic clove and squeeze the garlic out. Place in a screw-top jar with the vinegar, chopped basil and remaining oil and shake well to combine. Add the tomatoes and their juices, bacon and avocado to the fettuccine, pour on the dressing and toss well. Garnish with a few basil leaves and serve.

Serves 4

Note: Short-cut bacon is the meaty end of the bacon rasher and is also sold as eye bacon.

## Angel hair pasta with garlic, scallops and rocket

20 large scallops with roe
250 g (9 oz) angel hair pasta
150 ml (5 fl oz) extra virgin olive oil
2 garlic cloves, finely chopped
3 tablespoons white wine
1 tablespoon lemon juice
100 g (3½ oz) baby rocket (arugula)
1 very small handful coriander
  (cilantro) leaves

Pull or trim any veins, membrane or hard white muscle from the scallops. Pat the scallops dry with paper towels. Cook the pasta in a large saucepan of rapidly boiling salted water until al dente. Drain and transfer to a bowl. Toss with 1 tablespoon of the oil.

Meanwhile, heat 1 tablespoon oil in a frying pan, add the garlic and cook for a few seconds, or until fragrant. Do not brown. Add the wine and lemon juice, and remove from the heat.

Heat a chargrill pan or barbecue grill plate over high heat and brush with a little oil. Season the scallops and cook for 1 minute each side, or until just cooked.

Gently reheat the garlic mixture, add the rocket and stir over medium heat for 1–2 minutes, or until wilted. Toss through the pasta and mix together well. Add the remaining oil and half the coriander and mix well. Divide the pasta among bowls, arrange the scallops over the top and garnish with the remaining coriander.

Serves 4

Variation: Add ½ teaspoon chilli flakes just before the wine and lemon juice for an added kick.

## Tagliatelle with tuna, capers and rocket

350 g (12 oz) fresh tagliatelle
3 garlic cloves, crushed
1 teaspoon finely grated lemon zest
80 ml (2½ fl oz/⅓ cup) extra virgin
    olive oil
500 g (1 lb 2 oz) tuna, cut into
    1.5 cm (⅝ inch) cubes
200 g (7 oz) rocket (arugula),
    roughly chopped
60 g (2¼ oz/⅓ cup) salted baby
    capers, rinsed and patted dry
3 tablespoons lemon juice
2 tablespoons finely chopped flat-leaf
    (Italian) parsley

Cook the pasta in a saucepan of boiling salted water until al dente.

Meanwhile, put the garlic, lemon zest and 1 tablespoon of the oil in a bowl with the tuna and gently mix. Season.

Heat a frying pan over high heat and sear the tuna for 30 seconds on each side. Add the rocket and capers and gently stir for 1 minute, or until the rocket has just wilted. Pour in the lemon juice and then remove from the heat.

Add the remaining oil to the hot pasta along with the tuna mixture and parsley. Season and gently toss.

Serves 4

## Creamy garlic prawn fettuccine

400 g (14 oz) fresh fettuccine
1 tablespoon olive oil
1 onion, finely chopped
3 garlic cloves, crushed
400 g (14 oz) tomatoes, seeded
  and chopped
3 tablespoons white wine
300 ml (10½ fl oz) pouring
  (whipping) cream
1 kg (2 lb 4 oz) raw medium prawns
  (shrimp), peeled, deveined with
  tails intact
1 small handful basil leaves, chopped

Cook the fettuccine in a large saucepan of rapidly boiling salted water until al dente. Drain well and return to the pan to keep warm.

Heat the oil in a large frying pan over medium–high heat and cook the onion and garlic, stirring, for 4–5 minutes, or until the onion is soft. Add the tomato and wine and cook for 3 minutes before adding the cream. Bring to the boil, then reduce the heat to medium–low and simmer for 5 minutes, or until it slightly thickens. Stir in the prawns, then simmer for 3–4 minutes, or until the prawns turn pink and are curled and cooked through. Toss with the pasta, gently stir in the basil, season and serve immediately.

Serves 4

## Fettuccine with sweet potato, feta and olives

1.5 kg (3 lb 5 oz) orange sweet
   potato, cut into small cubes
80 ml (2½ fl oz/⅓ cup) olive oil
4 garlic cloves, crushed
2 tablespoons butter
4 red onions, sliced into thin wedges
500 g (1 lb 2 oz) fresh plain
   or spinach fettuccine
400 g (14 oz) soft feta cheese, diced
200 g (7 oz) small black olives
2 large handfuls basil, torn
extra virgin olive oil, for drizzling

Preheat the oven to 200°C (400°F/ Gas 6). Place the sweet potato, oil and garlic in a bowl and toss to coat the sweet potato. Lay out the sweet potato in a roasting tin and roast for 15 minutes. Turn and roast for another 15 minutes, until tender and golden— make sure the sweet potato is not too soft or it will not hold its shape. Keep warm.

Meanwhile, melt the butter in a deep frying pan and cook the onion over low heat, stirring occasionally, for 25–30 minutes, or until soft and slightly caramelised.

Cook the pasta in a large saucepan of rapidly boiling salted water until al dente. Drain well and return to the pan. Add the onion to the pasta and toss together. Add the sweet potato, feta, olives and basil and gently toss. Serve drizzled with extra virgin olive oil.

Serves 6

## Spaghetti marinara

3 tablespoons white wine
3 tablespoons fish stock
1 garlic clove, crushed
12 black mussels, cleaned
375 g (13 oz) spaghetti
30 g (1 oz) butter
125 g (4½ oz) squid, cleaned
    and cut into rings
125 g (4½ oz) skinless blue-eye
    trevalla fillet, cut into bite-sized
    pieces
200 g (7 oz) raw prawns (shrimp),
    peeled and deveined
1 small handful flat-leaf (Italian)
    parsley leaves, chopped
200 g (7 oz) tinned clams, drained

*Tomato sauce*
2 tablespoons olive oil
1 onion, finely chopped
1 carrot, finely chopped
2 garlic cloves, crushed
400 g (14 oz) tinned chopped
    tomatoes
125 ml (4 fl oz/½ cup) white wine
1 teaspoon white sugar

To make the tomato sauce, heat the oil in a saucepan, cook the onion and carrot over medium heat for 10 minutes, or until lightly browned. Add the garlic, tomato, wine and sugar, bring to the boil, then gently simmer for 30 minutes, stirring occasionally.

Heat the wine, stock and garlic in a large saucepan. Add the mussels. Cover and shake the pan over high heat for 5 minutes. After 3 minutes, start removing any opened mussels and set them aside. After 5 minutes, discard any unopened mussels and reserve the cooking liquid.

Cook the pasta in a large saucepan of rapidly boiling salted water until al dente. Drain well and return to the pan to keep warm.

Meanwhile, melt the butter in a frying pan and stir-fry the squid, blue-eye and prawns in batches for 2 minutes, or until just cooked. Remove from the heat and add to the tomato sauce along with the reserved cooking liquid, mussels, parsley and clams. Gently heat through, then toss the sauce with the pasta and serve.

Serves 4

## Spicy eggplant spaghetti

300 g (10½ oz) spaghetti
125 ml (4 fl oz/½ cup) extra virgin
 olive oil
2 red chillies, thinly sliced
1 onion, finely chopped
3 garlic cloves, crushed
4 slices bacon, chopped
400 g (14 oz) eggplant (aubergine),
 diced
2 tablespoons balsamic vinegar
2 tomatoes, chopped
3 tablespoons shredded basil

Cook the pasta in a large saucepan of rapidly boiling salted water until al dente. Drain well and return to the pan to keep warm.

Heat 1 tablespoon of the oil in a large, deep frying pan and cook the chilli, onion, garlic and bacon over medium heat for 5 minutes, or until the onion is golden and the bacon browned. Remove from the pan and set aside.

Add half the remaining oil to the pan and cook the eggplant over high heat, tossing to brown on all sides. Remove and repeat with the remaining oil and eggplant. Return the bacon mixture and all the eggplant to the pan, add the vinegar, tomato and basil and cook until heated through. Season well.

Serve the spaghetti topped with the eggplant mixture.

Serves 4

## Spaghetti puttanesca

400 g (14 oz) spaghetti
2 tablespoons olive oil
1 onion, finely chopped
2 garlic cloves, thinly sliced
1 small red chilli, cored, seeded
  and sliced
6 anchovy fillets, finely chopped
400 g (14 oz) tinned chopped
  tomatoes
1 tablespoon fresh oregano, finely
  chopped
16 black olives, halved and pitted
2 tablespoons salted baby capers,
  rinsed and patted dry
1 handful basil leaves

Cook the pasta in a large saucepan of rapidly boiling salted water until al dente. Drain well and return to the pan to keep warm.

Heat the olive oil in a large saucepan over medium heat. Add the onion, garlic and chilli and cook for 8 minutes, or until the onion is soft. Add the anchovies and cook for a further 1 minute. Add the tomato, oregano, olive halves and capers and bring to the boil. Reduce the heat, season and simmer for 3 minutes.

Add the spaghetti to the sauce and toss together. Scatter the basil over the top.

Serves 4

## Lemon and date ziti

360 g (12¾ oz/2 cups) dried pitted
   dates, halved
375 ml (13 fl oz/1½ cups) port
375 g (13 oz) ziti (see Notes)
3 tablespoons balsamic vinegar
125 ml (4 fl oz/½ cup) olive oil
150 g (5½ oz) rocket (arugula)
rind from 3 preserved lemons
   (see Notes), rinsed and finely
   chopped

Place the dates and port in a pan.
Bring to the boil, reduce the heat
and simmer for 10 minutes. Strain
the dates, reserving the port. Set
aside to cool.

Cook the ziti in a large saucepan
of rapidly boiling salted water until
al dente. Drain, rinse in cold water
and drain again. Allow to cool.

Combing the balsamic vinegar,
reserved port and oil in a bowl.
Season with a little sugar, if necessary.

Toss the dressing through the pasta
with the dates, rocket and lemon rind.

Serves 4-6

Notes: Note: Ziti is a wide tubular
pasta. You could use fettuccine or
spaghetti. Preserved lemons can be
purchased at any good delicatessen or
specialty food shop. They are available
bottled. This salad is also wonderful
served warm.

## Fettuccine with zucchini

500 g (1 lb 2 oz) fettuccine or
   tagliatelle
60 g (2¼ oz) butter
2 garlic cloves, crushed
500 g (1 lb 2 oz) zucchini (courgettes),
   grated
75 g (2½ oz/¾ cup) grated parmesan
   cheese
250 ml (9 fl oz/1 cup) olive oil
16 basil leaves

Cook the pasta in a large saucepan of rapidly boiling salted water until al dente. Drain well and return to the pan to keep warm.

Meanwhile, heat the butter in a deep heavy-based saucepan over low heat until it is foaming. Add the garlic and cook for 1 minute. Add the zucchini and cook, stirring occasionally, for 1–2 minutes or until the zucchini has softened.

Add the sauce to the pasta. Add the parmesan cheese and toss well.

To make basil leaves crisp, heat the oil in a small frying pan, add two leaves at a time and cook for 1 minute or until crisp. Drain on paper towels. Serve with the pasta.

Serves 4–6

## Baked fettuccine

500 g (1 lb 2 oz) spinach fettuccine
60 g (2¼ oz) butter
1 onion, finely chopped
300 g (10½ oz) sour cream
250 ml (9 fl oz/1 cup) pouring
  (whipping) cream
¼ teaspoon ground nutmeg
60 g (2¼ oz) grated parmesan cheese
150 g (5½ oz/1 cup) grated
  mozzarella cheese

Preheat the oven to 180°C (350°F/
Gas 4). Cook the pasta in a large
saucepan of rapidly boiling salted
water until al dente. Drain well.

Meanwhile, melt the butter in a large
saucepan and cook the onion over
low heat until tender. Add the pasta.
Add the sour cream and toss well.
Simmer, stirring, until the pasta is
well coated.

Stir in the cream, nutmeg and half the
parmesan cheese and season well.
Pour into a greased ovenproof dish.
Sprinkle with the combined mozzarella
and remaining parmesan. Bake for
15 minutes, or until golden.

Serves 4–6

## Spaghetti tomato salad

500 g (1 lb 2 oz) spaghetti
1 very large handful basil leaves,
   thinly sliced
250 g (9 oz) cherry tomatoes, halved
1 garlic clove, crushed
60 g (2¼ oz/½ cup) chopped
   black olives
3 tablespoons olive oil
1 tablespoon balsamic vinegar
60 g (2¼ oz) grated parmesan cheese

Cook the pasta in a large saucepan
of rapidly boiling salted water until
al dente. Drain well and rinse under
cold water.

Mix together the basil, tomato, garlic,
olives, oil and vinegar. Leave for
5 minutes. Toss with the pasta.

Add the parmesan and season. Toss
well to serve.

Serves 4–6

## Spaghettini with asparagus and rocket

100 ml (3½ fl oz) extra virgin olive oil
16 thin asparagus spears, cut into
  5 cm (2 inch) lengths
375 g (13 oz) spaghettini
120 g (4¼ oz) rocket (arugula),
  shredded
2 small fresh red chillies, finely
  chopped
2 teaspoons finely grated lemon zest
1 garlic clove, finely chopped
100 g (3½ oz/1 cup) grated parmesan
  cheese
2 tablespoons lemon juice

Bring a large saucepan of water to the boil over medium heat. Add 1 tablespoon of the oil and a pinch of salt to the water and blanch the asparagus for 3–4 minutes. Remove the asparagus with a slotted spoon, refresh under cold water, drain and place in a bowl. Return the water to a rapid boil and add the spaghettini. Cook the pasta until al dente. Drain and return to the pan.

Meanwhile, add the rocket, chilli, lemon zest, garlic and two-thrirds of the parmesan to the asparagus and mix well. Add to the pasta, pour on the lemon juice and remaining olive oil and season. Stir well to evenly coat the pasta with the mixture. Divide among bowls, top with the remaining parmesan and serve.

Serves 4

Note: You can use other types of pasta such as tagliatelle, macaroni or fusili.

## Smoked chicken linguine

1 tablespoon olive oil
1 leek, thinly sliced
3 large garlic cloves, finely chopped
125 ml (4 fl oz/½ cup) dry white wine
300 g (10½ oz) Swiss brown
   mushrooms, sliced
2 teaspoons chopped thyme
300 ml (10½ fl oz) thickened
   (whipping) cream
2 smoked chicken breast fillets,
   thinly sliced (see Note)
350 g (12 oz) fresh linguine

Heat the oil in a saucepan. Add the leek and cook, stirring, over low heat for 3–4 minutes, or until soft. Add the garlic and cook for another minute. Pour in the wine and simmer for 2–3 minutes, or until the liquid has reduced by half.

Increase the heat to medium, add the mushrooms and thyme and cook for 5 minutes, or until any excess liquid has been absorbed, then add the cream and sliced chicken. Reduce the heat and simmer for 4–5 minutes, or until the sauce has slightly thickened.

Meanwhile, cook the pasta in a large saucepan of rapidly boiling salted water until al dente. Drain and divide among serving plates. Spoon on the sauce and serve.

Note: Buy smoked chicken at the deli section of good supermarkets.

Serves 4

## Spaghetti with smoked tuna and olives

800 g (1 lb 12 oz) vine-ripened
  tomatoes
375 g (13 oz) spaghetti
375 g (13 oz) tinned smoked tuna
  slices in oil
1 red onion, chopped
2 garlic cloves, crushed
1 teaspoon white sugar
150 g (5½ oz) black olives
2 tablespoons chopped basil
75 g (2½ oz/½ cup) crumbled feta
  cheese

Score a cross in the base of each tomato. Place the tomatoes in a bowl of boiling water for 1 minute, then plunge into cold water and peel the skin away from the cross. Cut in half and remove the seeds with a teaspoon. Roughly chop the flesh. Cook the pasta in a large saucepan of rapidly boiling salted water until al dente. Drain well and return to the pan to keep warm.

Drain the oil from the tuna slices, reserving 1 tablespoon. Heat the reserved oil in a large saucepan, add the onion and cook over low heat for 3–4 minutes, or until soft but not brown. Add the crushed garlic and cook for another minute, then add the chopped tomatoes and sugar. Cook over medium heat for 8–10 minutes, or until pulpy.

Add the tuna slices, olives and basil, stir well and cook for 2 minutes, or until warmed through. Toss through the spaghetti and season. Sprinkle with crumbled feta and serve.

Serves 4

## Tagliatelle with asparagus and herbs

500 g (1 lb 2 oz) tagliatelle
175 g (6 oz) asparagus
2 tablespoons butter
1 tablespoon chopped flat-leaf
  (Italian) parsley
1 tablespoon chopped basil
310 ml (10¾ fl oz/1¼ cups) pouring
  (whipping) cream
60 g (2¼ oz) grated parmesan cheese

Cook the pasta in a large saucepan of rapidly boiling salted water until al dente. Drain well and return to the pan to keep warm.

Meanwhile, snap the woody ends from the asparagus and cut the stems into short lengths. Heat the butter in a saucepan and stir the asparagus over medium heat for 2 minutes or until just tender.

Add the chopped parsley and basil, cream, season and cook for 2 minutes.

Add the parmesan to the sauce and stir well. Toss through the pasta and serve in warmed bowls.

Serves 4–6

# Spaghetti with chilli squid

500 g (1 lb 2 oz) squid
500 g (1 lb 2 oz) spaghetti
2 tablespoons olive oil
1 leek, chopped
2 garlic cloves, crushed
1–2 teaspoons chopped chilli
1/2 teaspoon cayenne pepper
425 g (15 oz) tinned chopped
   tomatoes
125 ml (4 fl oz/1/2 cup) fish stock
   (see Note)
1 tablespoon chopped basil
2 teaspoons chopped sage
1 teaspoon chopped marjoram

Pull the tentacles from the squid bodies. Use your fingers to pull the quills away from the pouches. Pull the skin away from the flesh and discard. Using a sharp knife, slit the tubes up one side, lay out flat and score the inside in a diamond pattern. Cut each piece into four.

Cook the pasta in a large saucepan of rapidly boiling salted water until al dente. Drain well and return to the pan to keep warm.

Meanwhile, heat the oil in a large frying pan. Add the leek and cook for 2 minutes. Add the garlic and stir over low heat for 1 minute. Stir in the chilli and cayenne pepper. Add the tomato, stock and herbs. Bring to the boil. Reduce the heat and simmer for 5 minutes.

Add the squid to the sauce and simmer for another 5–10 minutes or until tender. Serve over the spaghetti.

Serves 4

Note: Make fish stock by putting fish bones and trimmings, 1 chopped onion, 1 celery stalk and 1 carrot in a large saucepan, and covering with cold water. Bring to the boil, then reduce the heat and simmer for 30 minutes. Drain well, discarding the solids, and use immediately.

## Tagliatelle with sweet tomato and walnut sauce

4 ripe Roma (plum) tomatoes
2 tablespoons olive oil
1 onion, finely chopped
1 celery stalk, finely chopped
1 carrot, grated
2 tablespoons chopped flat-leaf
  (Italian) parsley
1 teaspoon red wine vinegar
3 tablespoons dry white wine
500 g (1 lb 2 oz) tagliatelle
  or fettuccine
1 tablespoon olive oil, extra
90 g (3$^1$/$_4$ oz/$^3$/$_4$ cup) walnuts, roughly
  chopped
grated parmesan cheese, for serving

Score a cross on the base of each tomato, place in boiling water for 1 minute, then plunge into cold water. Peel the skin away from the cross and roughly chop the tomatoes.

Heat half of the oil in a large heavy-based saucepan and cook the onion and celery for 5 minutes over low heat, stirring regularly. Add the tomato, carrot, parsley and vinegar. Reduce the heat and simmer for 25 minutes. Season to taste.

Meanwhile, cook the pasta in a large saucepan of rapidly boiling salted water until al dente. Drain well and return to the pan to keep warm.

Heat the remaining oil in a frying pan and stir the walnuts over low heat for 5 minutes. Toss the pasta and sauce together and serve topped with walnuts and parmesan cheese.

Serves 4–6

## Baked spaghetti frittata

30 g (1 oz) butter
125 g (4½ oz) button mushrooms,
  sliced
1 red or green capsicum (pepper),
  seeded and chopped
125 g (4½ oz) ham, sliced
90 g (3¼ oz) frozen peas
6 eggs
250 ml (9 fl oz/1 cup) pouring
  (whipping) cream or milk
100 g (3½ oz) cooked spaghetti,
  chopped
2 tablespoons chopped flat-leaf
  (Italian) parsley
3 tablespoons grated parmesan
  cheese

Preheat the oven to 180°C (350°F/ Gas 4). Grease a 23 cm (9 inch) round ovenproof dish. Melt the butter in a frying pan and add the mushrooms. Cook over low heat for 2–3 minutes.

Add the capsicum and cook for 1 minute. Stir in the ham and peas. Remove from the heat to cool slightly.

Whisk together the eggs and cream and season. Add the spaghetti, parsley and mushroom mixture and stir. Pour into the dish and sprinkle with parmesan cheese. Bake for 25–30 minutes.

Serves 4

## Tagliatelle with asparagus, peas and herb sauce

375 g (13 oz) tagliatelle
2 leeks, thinly sliced
250 ml (9 fl oz/1 cup) chicken
    or vegetable stock
3 garlic cloves, crushed
250 g (9 oz/1½ cups) shelled
    fresh peas
1 tablespoon finely chopped mint
400 g (14 oz) asparagus spears,
    cut into 5 cm (2 inch) lengths
1 handful flat-leaf (Italian) parsley,
    finely chopped
1 handful basil, shredded
80 ml (2½ fl oz/⅓ cup) pouring
    (whipping) cream
pinch grated nutmeg
1 tablespoon grated parmesan cheese
2 tablespoons extra virgin olive oil,
    for serving

Cook the pasta in a large saucepan of rapidly boiling salted water until al dente. Drain well and return to the pan to keep warm.

Put the leeks and 125 ml (4 fl oz/ ½ cup) of the stock in a large, deep, frying pan. Cook over low heat, stirring often, for 4–5 minutes. Stir in the garlic, peas and mint and cook for 1 minute. Add the remaining stock and 125 ml (4 fl oz/½ cup) water and bring to the boil. Simmer for 5 minutes. Add the asparagus, parsley and basil and season well. Simmer for 3–4 minutes, or until the asparagus is just tender. Gradually increase the heat to thicken the sauce until it will just coat a spoon. Stir in the cream, nutmeg and parmesan and season.

Add the sauce to the tagliatelle and toss lightly to coat. Serve drizzled with the extra virgin olive oil.

Serves 4

## Linguine with broccoli, pine nuts and lemon

500 g (1 lb 2 oz) linguine
600 g (1 lb 5 oz) broccoli,
  cut into small florets
90 g (3¼ oz) pine nuts
125 ml (4 fl oz/½ cup) extra virgin
  olive oil
2 teaspoons finely grated lemon zest
3 tablespoons lemon juice
1 teaspoon chilli flakes
60 g (2¼ oz) grated parmesan cheese

Cook the pasta in a large saucepan of rapidly boiling salted water until al dente. Drain well and return to the pan to keep warm. Meanwhile, bring a saucepan of water to the boil and cook the broccoli for 2 minutes, or until just tender but still bright green. Drain and set aside.

Heat a large non-stick frying pan and dry-fry the pine nuts for 2–3 minutes, or until just golden, shaking the pan to prevent them burning. Remove from the pan and roughly chop. Reduce the heat to low, add the oil and lemon zest to the frying pan and gently heat until fragrant. Add the broccoli, chopped pine nuts, lemon juice and chilli and stir until warmed through. Season and add to the pasta with the parmesan and toss to combine. Divide among serving bowls.

Serves 4–6

## Spaghetti with creamy garlic mussels

500 g (1 lb 2 oz) spaghetti
1.5 kg (3 lb 5 oz) mussels
2 tablespoons olive oil
2 garlic cloves, crushed
125 ml (4 fl oz/½ cup) white wine
250 ml (9 fl oz/1 cup) pouring
  (whipping) cream
2 tablespoons chopped basil

Cook the spaghetti in a large saucepan of rapidly boiling salted water until al dente. Drain well and return to the pan to keep warm.

While the spaghetti is cooking, remove the beards from the mussels and scrub away any grit. Discard any open mussels. Set aside. Heat the oil in a large saucepan. Add the garlic and stir over low heat for 30 seconds.

Add the wine and mussels. Simmer, covered, for 5 minutes. Remove the mussels, discarding any that don't open, and set aside. Add the cream, basil and season. Simmer for 2 minutes, stirring occasionally. Serve the sauce and mussels over the spaghetti.

Serves 4

Curly

## Fusilli with roasted tomatoes, tapenade and bocconcini

800 g (1 lb 12 oz) cherry or teardrop
    tomatoes (or a mixture of both),
    halved if they are large
500 g (1 lb 2 oz) fusilli
300 g (10½ oz) bocconcini (baby
    mozzarella cheese), sliced
1 tablespoon chopped thyme

*Tapenade*
1½ tablespoons salted capers,
    rinsed and patted dry
2 small garlic cloves
185 g (6½ oz/1½ cups) sliced
    black olives
3 tablespoons lemon juice
80–100 ml (2½–3½ fl oz) extra virgin
    olive oil

Preheat the oven to 200°C (400°F/
Gas 6). Place the tomatoes on a
baking tray, sprinkle with salt and
pepper and bake for 10 minutes,
or until slightly dried.

To make the tapenade, place the
capers, garlic, olives and lemon juice
in a food processor and mix together.
With the motor running, gradually
add the oil until the mixture forms
a smooth paste.

Cook the pasta in a large saucepan
of rapidly boiling water until al dente,
then drain.

Toss the tapenade and bocconcini
through the hot pasta. Top with the
roasted tomatoes and thyme and
serve immediately.

Serves 4–6

## Warm minted chicken and pasta salad

250 g (9 oz) cotelli pasta
125 ml (4 fl oz/½ cup) olive oil
1 large red capsicum (pepper)
3 chicken breast fillets
6 spring onions (scallions),
  cut into 2 cm (¾ inch) lengths
4 garlic cloves, thinly sliced
1 handful mint leaves, chopped
80 ml (2½ fl oz/⅓ cup) cider vinegar
100 g (3½ oz) baby spinach leaves

Cook the pasta in a large saucepan of boiling water until al dente, drain, stir in 1 tablespoon of the oil and set aside.

Meanwhile, cut the capsicum into quarters, removing the seeds and membrane. Place, skin side up, under a hot grill (broiler) for 8–10 minutes, or until the skin blackens and blisters. Cool in a plastic bag, then peel away the skin. Cut into thin strips. Place the chicken between two sheets of plastic wrap and slightly flatten.

Heat 1 tablespoon of the oil in a large frying pan, add the chicken and cook over medium heat for 2–3 minutes each side, or until light brown and cooked through. Remove from the pan and cut into 5 mm (⅛ inch) slices.

Add another tablespoon of the oil to the pan and add the spring onion, sliced garlic and capsicum and cook, stirring, for 2–3 minutes, or until starting to soften. Add two-thirds of the mint, the vinegar and the remaining oil and stir until warmed through. In a large bowl, combine the pasta, chicken, spinach, onion mixture and remaining mint and toss well, season and serve warm.

Serves 4

## Lamb and pasta soup

2 tablespoons olive oil
500 g (1 lb 2 oz) lean lamb,
    cut into bite-sized cubes
2 onions, finely chopped
2 carrots, chopped
4 celery stalks, chopped
425 g (15 oz) tinned chopped
    tomatoes
2 litres (70 fl oz/8 cups) beef stock
300 g (10½ oz) fusilli
chopped flat-leaf (Italian) parsley,
    for serving

Heat the oil in a large saucepan and cook the lamb in batches until golden brown. Remove each batch as it is cooked and drain on paper towels. Add the onion to the pan and cook for 2 minutes or until softened. Return all the meat to the pan.

Add the carrot, celery, tomato and beef stock. Stir to combine and bring to the boil. Reduce the heat to low and simmer, covered, for 15 minutes.

Add the fusilli to the soup. Stir briefly to prevent the pasta sticking to the pan. Simmer, uncovered, for another 15 minutes or until the lamb and pasta are tender. Sprinkle with chopped parsley before serving.

Serves 6–8

Hint: If you prefer, the pasta can be cooked separately, drained and added to the soup just before serving.

Variations: For a lighter flavour, use half stock and half water. Vegetable stock can be used instead of beef.

## Prosciutto and vegetable pasta bake

3 tablespoons olive oil
35 g (1¼ oz/⅓ cup) dried
  breadcrumbs
250 g (9 oz) pasta shapes
6 thin slices prosciutto, chopped
1 red onion, chopped
1 red capsicum (pepper), chopped
100 g (3½ oz/½ cup) semi-dried
  (sun-blushed) tomatoes,
  roughly chopped
3 tablespoons shredded basil
100 g (3½ oz/1 cup) grated
  parmesan cheese
4 eggs, lightly beaten
250 ml (9 fl oz/1 cup) milk

Preheat the oven to 180°C (350°F/ Gas 4). Grease a 25 cm (10 inch) round ovenproof dish with a little of the olive oil and sprinkle the dish with 2 tablespoons of the breadcrumbs to coat the base and side. Cook the pasta in a large saucepan of boiling water until al dente. Drain and transfer to a large bowl.

Heat 1 tablespoon of the remaining oil in a large frying pan. Add the prosciutto and onion and cook over medium heat for 4–5 minutes, or until softened and golden in colour. Add the capsicum and semi-dried tomato and cook for a further 1–2 minutes. Add to the pasta with the basil and parmesan and toss together. Spoon the mixture into the prepared dish.

Place the eggs and milk in a bowl, whisk together, then season. Pour the egg mixture over the pasta. Season the remaining breadcrumbs, add the remaining oil and toss together. Sprinkle the seasoned breadcrumb mixture over the pasta. Bake for 40 minutes, or until set. Allow to stand for 5 minutes, then cut into wedges and serve with a green salad, if desired.

Serves 6–8

## Cotelli with spring vegetables

500 g (1 lb 2 oz) cotelli pasta
310 g (11 oz/2 cups) frozen peas
310 g (11 oz/2 cups) frozen broad
(fava) beans, blanched and peeled
80 ml (2½ fl oz/⅓ cup) olive oil
6 spring onions (scallions), cut into
3 cm (1¼ inch) pieces
2 garlic cloves, finely chopped
250 ml (9 fl oz/1 cup) chicken stock
12 thin fresh asparagus spears, cut
into 5 cm (2 inch) lengths
juice and finely grated zest of 1 lemon
shaved parmesan cheese, for serving

Cook the cotelli in a large saucepan of rapidly boiling salted water until al dente. Drain and return to the pan to keep warm.

Meanwhile, cook the peas in a saucepan of boiling water for 1–2 minutes, until tender. Remove with a slotted spoon and plunge into cold water. Add the broad beans to the saucepan, cook for 1–2 minutes, then drain and plunge into cold water. Remove and slip the skins off.

Heat 2 tablespoons of the oil in a frying pan. Add the spring onion and garlic and cook over medium heat for 2 minutes, or until softened. Pour in the stock and cook for 5 minutes, or until slightly reduced. Add the asparagus and cook for 3–4 minutes, until bright green and just tender. Stir in the peas and broad beans and cook for 2–3 minutes, or until heated through.

Toss the remaining oil through the pasta, then add the vegetable mixture, lemon zest and juice. Season and toss together well. Divide among bowls and top with shaved parmesan.

Serves 4

## Fusilli salad with sherry vinaigrette

300 g (10½ oz) fusilli
250 g (9 oz/2 cups) cauliflower florets
125 ml (4 fl oz/½ cup) olive oil
16 slices pancetta
1 small handful sage leaves
100 g (3½ oz/⅔ cup) pine nuts,
    toasted
2 tablespoons finely chopped red
    shallots
1½ tablespoons sherry vinegar
1 small red chilli, finely chopped
2 garlic cloves, crushed
1 teaspoon soft brown sugar
2 tablespoons orange juice
1 small handful flat-leaf (Italian)
    parsley leaves, finely chopped
35 g (1¼ oz/⅓ cup) shaved parmesan
    cheese

Cook the fusilli in a large saucepan of rapidly boiling, salted water for 12 minutes, or until al dente. Drain and refresh under cold water until it is cool. Drain well. Blanch the cauliflower florets in boiling water for 3 minutes, then drain and cool.

Heat 1 tablespoon of olive oil in a non-stick frying pan and cook the pancetta for 2 minutes or until crisp. Drain on crumpled paper towels. Add 1 more tablespoon of oil and cook the sage leaves for 1 minute or until crisp. Drain on crumpled paper towels. In a large serving bowl, combine the pasta, pine nuts and cauliflower.

Heat the remaining olive oil, add the shallots and cook gently for 2 minutes, or until soft. Remove from the heat then add the vinegar, chilli, garlic, brown sugar, orange juice and chopped parsley. Pour the warm dressing over the pasta and toss gently to combine.

Place the salad in a serving bowl. Crumble the pancetta over the top and scatter with sage leaves and shaved parmesan. Serve warm.

Serves 6

## Speedy chicken and pasta bake

200 g (7 oz) fusilli
425 g (15 oz) tinned cream of
  mushroom or broccoli soup
250 g (9 oz/1 cup) sour cream
1 teaspoon curry powder
1 barbecued chicken
250 g (9 oz) broccoli, cut into florets
90 g (3 1/4 oz) fresh breadcrumbs
185 g (6 1/2 oz/1 1/2 cups) grated
  cheddar cheese

Preheat the oven to 180°C (350°F/ Gas 4). Cook the pasta in a large saucepan of rapidly boiling salted water until al dente. Drain well and return to the pan to keep warm.

Combine the soup, sour cream and curry powder and season.

Remove the meat from the chicken and roughly chop. Combine the chicken with the pasta, broccoli and soup mixture. Spoon into lightly greased 500 ml (17 fl oz/2 cup) ovenproof dishes and sprinkle with the combined breadcrumbs and cheese. Bake for 25–30 minutes, or until the cheese melts.

Serves 4

Variation: This recipe can be made in a 2 litre (70 fl oz/8 cup) ovenproof dish and baked for 40 minutes, or until the cheese has melted.

## Pasta with creamy tomato and bacon sauce

400 g (14 oz) curly pasta, such as
  cresti di gallo (see Notes)
1 tablespoon olive oil
175 g (6 oz) streaky bacon, thinly
  sliced (see Notes)
500 g (1 lb 2 oz) Roma (plum)
  tomatoes, roughly chopped
125 ml (4 fl oz/1/2 cup) thick
  (double/heavy) cream
2 tablespoons sun-dried tomato pesto
2 tablespoons finely chopped flat-leaf
  (Italian) parsley
50 g (1¾ oz/1/2 cup) grated
  parmesan cheese

Cook the pasta in a large saucepan of boiling salted water until al dente. Drain and return to the saucepan.

Meanwhile, heat the oil in a frying pan, add the bacon and cook over high heat for 2 minutes, or until starting to brown. Reduce the heat to medium, add the tomato and cook, stirring frequently, for 2 minutes, or until the tomato has softened but still holds its shape.

Add the cream and tomato pesto and stir until heated through. Remove from the heat, add the parsley and then toss the sauce through the pasta with the grated parmesan.

Serves 4

Notes: Cresti di gallo pasta is named after the Italian word for 'cockscombs' because of its similarity to the crest of a rooster. Streaky bacon is the tail fatty end of bacon. It is fattier but adds to the flavour of the meal. You can use 175 g (6 oz) regular bacon, if you prefer.

## Pasta and white bean soup

185 g (6½ oz) fusilli
1.5 litres (52 fl oz/6 cups) chicken
  stock
600 g (1 lb 5 oz) tinned white beans,
  drained and rinsed

*Pesto*
50 g (1¾ oz/⅓ cup) pine nuts
2 large handfuls basil leaves
50 g (1¾ oz) rocket (arugula)
2 garlic cloves, chopped
35 g (1¼ oz/⅓ cup) grated
  parmesan cheese
80 ml (2½ fl oz/⅓ cup) olive oil

To make the pesto, put the pine nuts in a dry frying pan and toast them over medium heat for 1–2 minutes, or until golden brown. Remove from the pan and allow to cool. Mix the pine nuts, basil, rocket, garlic and parmesan in a food processor and process until finely chopped. With the motor running, add the oil in a thin stream until well combined. Season and set aside.

Cook the pasta in a large saucepan of rapidly boiling salted water until al dente. Drain well and return to the pan to keep warm.

Heat the chicken stock in a large saucepan until it begins to boil. Reduce the heat to simmering point. Add the pasta and beans to the stock. Reheat and serve with a spoonful of pesto.

Serves 6

## Fusilli with tuna, capers and parsley

425 g (15 oz) tinned tuna in spring
  water, drained
2 tablespoons olive oil
2 garlic cloves, finely chopped
2 small red chillies, finely chopped
3 tablespoons salted capers, rinsed
  and patted dry
1 small handful flat-leaf (Italian) parsley
  leaves, chopped
3 tablespoons lemon juice
375 g (13 oz) fusilli
125 ml (4 fl oz/½ cup) hot chicken
  stock

Put the tuna in a bowl and flake it
lightly with a fork. Combine the oil,
garlic, chilli, capers, parsley and lemon
juice in a small bowl. Pour the mixture
over the tuna and mix lightly. Season.

Meanwhile, cook the pasta in a large
saucepan of rapidly boiling salted
water until al dente. Drain. Toss the
tuna mixture through the pasta,
adding enough of the hot chicken
stock to make it moist—you may
not need it all.

Serves 4

## Peppered pork, zucchini and garganelli

450 g (1 lb) pork fillet
3–4 teaspoons cracked black
  peppercorns
80 g (2¾ oz) butter
250 g (9 oz) garganelli pasta
1 onion, halved and thinly sliced
2 large zucchini (courgettes),
  thinly sliced
1 large handful basil leaves, torn
155 g (5½ oz/¾ cup) small black
  olives
60 g (2¼ oz/½ cup) grated
  Romano cheese

Cut the pork fillet in half widthways and roll in the pepper and some salt. Heat half the butter in a large deep frying pan, add the pork and cook for 4 minutes on each side, or until golden brown and just cooked through. Remove from the pan and cut into 5 mm (¼ inch) slices, then set aside and keep warm.

Cook the pasta in a large saucepan of boiling water until al dente; drain well and return to the pan.

Meanwhile, melt the remaining butter in the frying pan, add the onion and cook, stirring, over medium heat for about 3 minutes, or until soft. Add the zucchini and toss for 5 minutes, or until starting to soften. Add the basil, olives, sliced pork and any juices and toss well. Stir the pork mixture through the hot pasta, then season. Serve immediately topped with the cheese.

*Serves 4*

## Simple vegetable and pasta soup

2 teaspoons olive oil
1 onion, chopped
1 carrot, chopped
2 celery stalks, chopped
350 g (12 oz) orange sweet potato,
  chopped
400 g (14 oz) tinned corn kernels,
  drained
1 litre (35 fl oz/4 cups) vegetable stock
90 g (3¼ oz/1 cup) fusilli

Heat the oil in a large saucepan
and add the onion, carrot and celery.
Cook over low heat, stirring regularly,
for 10 minutes, or until soft.

Add the sweet potato, corn kernels
and stock. Bring to the boil, reduce
the heat and simmer for 20 minutes,
or until the vegetables are tender.

Add the pasta to the pan and return
to the boil. Reduce the heat and
simmer for 10 minutes, or until the
pasta is al dente. Serve immediately.

Serves 6

## Cotelli, tomato and artichoke grill

350 g (12 oz) cotelli
285 g (10 oz) marinated artichoke
  hearts, drained and chopped
2 tablespoons olive oil
250 ml (9 fl oz/1 cup) pouring
  (whipping) cream
2 tablespoons chopped thyme
2 garlic cloves, crushed
75 g (2½ oz/¾ cup) grated parmesan
  cheese
210 g (7½ oz/1⅔ cups) grated
  cheddar cheese
950 g (2 lb 2 oz) tomatoes, cut into
  5 mm (¼ inch) slices

Cook the pasta in a large saucepan of rapidly boiling salted water until al dente. Drain well and return to the pan to keep warm.

Lightly grease a 23 cm x 30 cm (9 inch x 12 inch) rectangular ovenproof dish. Stir the artichokes, olive oil, cream, thyme, garlic, half the parmesan and 155 g (5½ oz/ 1¼ cups) of the cheddar through the pasta and season. Spread evenly in the dish.

Arrange the tomatoes over the top, overlapping one another. Season, then sprinkle with the remaining cheese. Cook under a hot grill (broiler) for 6 minutes, or until the cheeses melt and are golden brown.

Serves 4

## Pasta with chicken, mushroom and tarragon

375 g (13 oz) fusilli
2 tablespoons virgin olive oil
350 g (12 oz) chicken tenderloins,
  cut into 2 cm (3/4 inch) pieces
20 g (3/4 oz) butter
400 g (14 oz) Swiss brown or button
  mushrooms, sliced
2 garlic cloves, finely chopped
125 ml (4 fl oz/1/2 cup) dry white wine
185 ml (6 fl oz/3/4 cup) pouring
  (whipping) cream
1 teaspoon finely grated lemon zest
2 tablespoons lemon juice
1 tablespoon chopped tarragon
2 tablespoons chopped flat-leaf
  (Italian) parsley
3 tablespoons grated parmesan
  cheese, plus extra for serving

Cook the pasta in a large saucepan of rapidly boiling salted water until al dente. Drain well and return to the pan to keep warm.

Meanwhile, heat 1 tablespoon of the oil in a large frying pan, add the chicken and cook over high heat for 3–4 minutes, or until lightly browned. Remove from the pan.

Heat the butter and the remaining oil, add the mushrooms and cook, stirring, over high heat for 3 minutes. Add the garlic and cook for a further 2 minutes.

Pour in the wine, then reduce the heat to low and simmer for 5 minutes, or until nearly evaporated. Add the cream and chicken and simmer for about 5 minutes, or until thickened.

Stir the lemon zest, lemon juice, tarragon, parsley and parmesan into the sauce. Season, then add the hot pasta, tossing until well combined. Serve with the extra parmesan.

Serves 4

## Fusilli with broccolini, chilli and olives

3 tablespoons olive oil
1 onion, finely chopped
3 garlic cloves
1 teaspoon chilli flakes
700 g (1 lb 9 oz) broccolini, cut into
  1 cm (½ inch) pieces
125 ml (4 fl oz/½ cup) vegetable stock
400 g (14 oz) fusilli
90 g (3¼ oz/½ cup) black olives,
  pitted and chopped
3 tablespoons finely chopped flat-leaf
  (Italian) parsley
3 tablespoons grated pecorino cheese
2 tablespoons basil leaves, shredded

Heat the olive oil in a large non-stick frying pan over medium heat. Cook the onion, garlic and chilli until softened, then add the broccolini and cook for 5 minutes. Pour in the stock and cook, covered, for 5 minutes.

Meanwhile, cook the fusilli in a large saucepan of rapidly boiling water until al dente. Drain and keep warm.

When the broccolini is tender, remove from the heat. Add to the pasta with the olives, parsley, pecorino and basil, and season well. Gently toss together and serve immediately.

Serves 4

## Goulash with fusilli

400 g (14 oz) fusilli
2 tablespoons olive oil
1 large onion, sliced into thin wedges
600 g (1 lb 5 oz) rump steak, trimmed
    and cut into 2 cm (¾ inch) cubes
1 tablespoon plain (all-purpose) flour
1 small green capsicum (pepper),
    diced
850 g (1 lb 14 oz) tinned diced
    tomatoes
1 teaspoon hot paprika
80 g (2¾ oz/⅓ cup) light sour cream

Cook the pasta in a large saucepan of rapidly boiling salted water until al dente. Drain well and return to the pan to keep warm.

Meanwhile, heat 1 tablespoon of the olive oil in a large frying pan over medium heat. Add the onion and cook, stirring, for 4–5 minutes, or until softened and golden. Remove the onion from the pan.

Heat the remaining olive oil in the same frying pan over high heat. Toss the steak cubes in the flour, shaking off any excess, then add to the pan and cook for 2 minutes to brown on all sides. Add the capsicum, tomato, paprika and the cooked onion and stir to combine.

Bring the mixture to the boil, then reduce the heat and simmer for 8–10 minutes, stirring occasionally. Season. To serve, spoon the goulash mixture over the pasta and top with sour cream.

Serves 4

## Ratatouille and pasta soup

1 eggplant (aubergine), chopped
1 tablespoon olive oil
1 large onion, chopped
1 large red capsicum (pepper),
    chopped
1 large green capsicum (pepper),
    chopped
2 garlic cloves, crushed
3 zucchini (courgettes), sliced
800 g (1 lb 12 oz) tinned chopped
    tomatoes
1 teaspoon dried oregano
½ teaspoon dried thyme
1 litre (35 fl oz/4 cups) vegetable stock
45 g (1½ oz) cotelli pasta
grated parmesan cheese, for serving

Spread the eggplant out in a colander and sprinkle generously with salt. Leave for 20 minutes; rinse and pat dry with paper towels.

Heat the oil in a large heavy-based saucepan and cook the onion for 10 minutes, or until soft and lightly golden. Add the capsicum, garlic, zucchini and eggplant and cook for 5 minutes.

Add the tomato, herbs and stock to the pan. Bring to the boil, then reduce the heat and simmer for 10 minutes, or until the vegetables are tender. Add the pasta and cook for 15 minutes, until al dente. Serve with parmesan.

Serves 6

## Sweet potato, rocket and walnut pasta salad

800 g (1 lb 12 oz) orange sweet
 potato, cut into 2 cm (3/4 inch) cubes
150 ml (5 fl oz) olive oil
125 g (4 1/2 oz/1 cup) walnut pieces
350 g (12 oz) fricelli pasta
150 g (5 1/2 oz) white castello cheese
 (or other creamy soft-rind cheese),
 softened
2 garlic cloves, crushed
2 teaspoons lemon juice
1/2 teaspoon white sugar
100 g (3 1/2 oz) baby rocket (arugula)

Preheat the oven to 200°C (400°F/ Gas 6). Toss the sweet potato in 2 tablespoons of the oil and place in a single layer on a baking tray lined with baking paper. Season. Roast, turning halfway through, for 30 minutes, or until golden and cooked through.

Spread the walnuts on a baking tray and roast for 10 minutes, or until crisp.

Meanwhile, cook the pasta in a large saucepan of boiling salted water until al dente. Drain well and return to the pan to keep warm.

Remove the rind from one-third of the cheese and cut the rest into cubes. Finely chop 2 tablespoons of the walnuts. Combine with the garlic, lemon juice, sugar, remaining oil and rindless cheese. Season. Combine the pasta, sweet potato, rocket, cubed cheese and remaining walnuts in a bowl. Drizzle with the dressing and toss together. Season.

Serves 4

## Chicken, broccoli and pasta bake

300 g (10½ oz) fricelli pasta
425 g (15 oz) tinned cream
  of mushroom soup
2 eggs
185 g (6½ oz/¾ cup) mayonnaise
1 tablespoon Dijon mustard
200 g (7 oz) grated cheddar cheese
600 g (1 lb 5 oz) chicken breast fillets,
  thinly sliced
400 g (14 oz) broccoli florets
40 g (1½ oz/½ cup) fresh
  breadcrumbs

Preheat the oven to 180°C (350°F/ Gas 4). Cook the pasta in a large saucepan of rapidly boiling salted water until al dente. Drain well and return to the pan to keep warm.

Combine the soup, eggs, mayonnaise, mustard and half the cheese in a bowl.

Heat a lightly greased non-stick frying pan over medium heat, add the chicken and cook for 5–6 minutes, or until cooked through. Season and set aside to cool.

Add the chicken and broccoli to the pasta. Pour the soup mixture over the top and stir. Transfer the mixture to a 3 litre ovenproof dish. Sprinkle with combined breadcrumbs and remaining cheese. Bake for 20 minutes, or until golden brown.

Serves 6–8

## Italian omelette

2 tablespoons olive oil
1 onion, finely chopped
155 g (5½ oz/1 cup) sliced ham,
  chopped
6 eggs
3 tablespoons milk
350 g (12 oz/2 cups) cooked fusilli
  (see Note)
3 tablespoons grated parmesan
  cheese
2 tablespoons chopped flat-leaf
  (Italian) parsley
1 tablespoon chopped basil
60 g (2¼ oz/½ cup) grated cheddar
  cheese

Heat half the oil in a frying pan. Add the onion and stir over low heat until tender. Add the ham and stir for 1 minute. Transfer to a plate.

Whisk together the eggs and milk and season. Stir in the pasta, parmesan, herbs and onion mixture.

Preheat the grill (broiler) to hot. Heat the remaining oil in the same pan. Pour the egg mixture into the pan. Sprinkle with the cheddar cheese. Cook over medium heat until the omelette begins to set around the edges, then place under the grill until lightly browned on top. Cut into wedges for serving.

Note: To get 2 cups of cooked pasta you will need to start with about 150 g (5½ oz) of dried pasta.

Serves 4

## Fusilli with bacon and broad bean sauce

500 g (1 lb 2 oz) fusilli or penne
310 g (11 oz/2 cups) frozen broad
    (fava) beans
2 tablespoons olive oil
2 leeks, thinly sliced
4 slices bacon, diced
310 ml (10¾ fl oz/1¼ cups) pouring
    (whipping) cream
2 teaspoons finely grated lemon zest

Cook the pasta in a large saucepan of rapidly boiling salted water until al dente. Drain well and return to the pan to keep warm.

While the pasta is cooking, plunge the broad beans into a saucepan of boiling water. Remove with a slotted spoon and place immediately in cold water. Drain, allow to cool, then peel.

Heat the oil in a heavy-based frying pan. Add the leek and bacon and cook over medium heat, stirring occasionally, for 8 minutes, or until the leek is golden. Add the cream and lemon zest and cook for 2 minutes. Add the broad beans and season well.

Add the sauce to the pasta and toss to combine. Serve at once.

Serves 4–6

# Beef sausage pasta

150 g (5½ oz) fusilli
4 thick beef sausages
2 tablespoons olive oil
1 large red onion, cut into wedges
250 ml (9 oz/1 cup) Italian tomato
  pasta sauce
4 small ripe tomatoes, peeled,
  seeded and chopped
2 tablespoons chopped flat-leaf
  (Italian) parsley

Cook the pasta in a large saucepan of rapidly boiling salted water until al dente. Drain well and return to the pan to keep warm, reserving 3 tablespoons of the cooking water.

Meanwhile, prick the sausages all over with a fork. Heat a non-stick frying pan and cook the sausages over medium heat, turning often, for 5 minutes, or until cooked. Cut into thick diagonal slices and set aside.

Clean the frying pan and heat the oil. Cook the onion wedges over medium heat for 3 minutes, or until soft. Add the tomato pasta sauce and the tomato. Cook for 5 minutes, or until the tomato has softened. Add the sliced sausage and heat through for 1 minute.

Toss the pasta through the sauce, adding a little of the reserved pasta water, if necessary. Sprinkle with parsley and serve.

Serves 4

## Cotelli with capers, bocconcini and basil oil

125 ml (4 fl oz/1/2 cup) olive oil
125 g (41/2 oz) capers in brine,
  drained, rinsed and patted dry
500 g (1 lb 2 oz) cotelli pasta
2 tablespoons lemon juice
3 large handfuls basil leaves
35 g (11/4 oz/1/3 cup) grated parmesan
  cheese
250 g (9 oz) cherry tomatoes,
  quartered
8 bocconcini (baby mozzarella
  cheese), quartered
extra virgin olive oil, for serving

Heat half the olive oil in a frying pan, add the capers and cook over high heat for 3–4 minutes, or until crisp and golden. Drain on paper towels and set aside.

Cook the pasta in a large saucepan of rapidly boiling salted water until al dente. Drain well and return to the pan to keep warm.

Meanwhile, mix the lemon juice, 2 large handfuls of the basil and the remaining olive oil in a food processor until smooth. Season.

Roughly tear the remaining basil leaves, then toss through the warm pasta with the basil mixture, 2 tablespoons of the parmesan and the cherry tomatoes. Spoon into warmed bowls and top with the bocconcini and capers. Drizzle with the extra virgin olive oil and garnish with the remaining grated parmesan.

Serves 4–6

# Flat

# Fresh vegetable lasagne with rocket

16 asparagus spears, trimmed and
   cut into 5 cm (2 inch) lengths
150 g (5½ oz/1 cup) fresh or frozen
   peas
2 large zucchini (courgettes),
   cut into thin ribbons
2 fresh lasagne sheets
   (each sheet 24 cm x 35 cm/
   9½ inches x 14 inches)
100 g (3½ oz) rocket (arugula)
1 large handful basil leaves, torn
2 tablespoons extra virgin olive oil
250 g (9 oz/1 cup) low-fat ricotta
150 g (5½ oz) semi-dried
   (sun-blushed) tomatoes
parmesan shavings, for garnishing

*Balsamic syrup*
80 ml (2½ fl oz/⅓ cup) balsamic
   vinegar
1½ tablespoons brown sugar

To make the syrup, stir the vinegar
and brown sugar in a small saucepan
over medium heat until the sugar
dissolves. Reduce the heat and
simmer for 3–4 minutes, or until the
sauce becomes syrupy. Remove
from the heat.

Bring a large saucepan of salted water
to the boil. Blanch the asparagus,
peas and zucchini in separate batches
until just tender, refreshing each
batch in cold water. Return the
cooking liquid to the boil. Cook the
lasagne sheets in the boiling water for
1–2 minutes, or until al dente. Refresh
in cold water and drain well. Cut each
sheet in half lengthways.

Toss the vegetables and the rocket
with the basil and olive oil. Season.
To assemble, place one strip of pasta
on a plate—one-third on the centre of
the plate and two-thirds overhanging
one side. Place a small amount of the
salad on the centre one-third, topped
with some ricotta and tomato. Season
lightly and fold over one-third of the
lasagne sheet. Top with a layer of
salad, ricotta and tomato. Fold back
the final layer of pasta and garnish
with salad and tomato. Repeat with
the remaining pasta, salad, ricotta
and tomato. Drizzle with the syrup
and garnish with parmesan.

Serves 4

## Roast pumpkin sauce on pappardelle

1.4 kg butternut pumpkin (squash),
cut into 2 cm pieces
4 garlic cloves, crushed
3 teaspoons fresh thyme leaves
100 ml (3½ fl oz) olive oil
500 g (17 oz) pappardelle pasta
2 tablespoons cream
185 ml (6 fl oz/¾ cup) hot chicken
stock
30 g (1 oz) shaved Parmesan

Preheat the oven to 200°C (400°F/ Gas 6). Place the pumpkin, garlic, thyme and 60 ml (2 fl oz/¼ cup) olive oil in a bowl and toss together. Then season with salt. Transfer to a baking tray and cook for 30 minutes, or until tender and golden.

Meanwhile, cook the pasta in a large saucepan of boiling water until al dente. Drain and return to the pan. Toss through the remaining oil and keep warm.

Place the cooked pumpkin and cream in a food processor and process until smooth. Add the hot stock and then process until combined and smooth. Season with salt and cracked black pepper and gently toss through the pasta. Divide onto four serving plates, sprinkle with Parmesan and thyme, if desired, and serve immediately.

Serves 4

Note: The sauce becomes gluggy on standing, so serve it as soon as possible.

## Lasagnette with spicy chicken meatballs

750 g (1 lb 10 oz) minced (ground)
  chicken
2 tablespoons chopped coriander
  (cilantro) leaves
1½ tablespoons red curry paste
2 tablespoons oil
1 red onion, finely chopped
3 garlic cloves, crushed
875 ml (30 fl oz/3½ cups) Italian
  tomato pasta sauce
2 teaspoons soft brown sugar
350 g (12 oz) lasagnette

Line a tray with baking paper. Combine the meat, coriander and 1 tablespoon of the curry paste. Roll heaped tablespoons of the mixture into balls and put on the tray. Refrigerate.

Heat the oil in a large deep frying pan over medium heat. Cook the onion and garlic for 2–3 minutes, or until softened. Add the remaining curry paste and cook, stirring, for 1 minute, or until fragrant. Add the pasta sauce and sugar and stir well. Reduce the heat and add the meatballs. Cook, turning halfway through, for 10 minutes, or until the meatballs are cooked through.

Meanwhile, cook the pasta in a large saucepan of boiling salted water until al dente. Drain well and return to the pan to keep warm.

Serve topped with the sauce and meatballs. Garnish with coriander, if desired.

Serves 4

## Tuna and chermoula on pappardelle

500 g (1 lb 2 oz) orange sweet potato, cut into 2 cm (¾ inch) cubes
100 ml (3½ fl oz) olive oil
1 large handful coriander (cilantro) leaves, finely chopped
1 small handful flat-leaf (Italian) parsley leaves, chopped
3 garlic cloves, crushed
3 teaspoons ground cumin
3 tablespoons lemon juice
4 x 180 g (6 oz) tuna steaks
400 g (14 oz) pappardelle

Preheat the oven to 200°C (400°F/ Gas 6). Toss the sweet potato in 2 tablespoons of the oil. Place on a baking tray and roast for 25–30 minutes, or until tender.

To make the chermoula, put the coriander, parsley, garlic, cumin and ¾ teaspoon freshly ground black pepper in a small food processor and process until a rough paste forms. Transfer to a bowl and stir in the lemon juice and 1 tablespoon oil.

Put the tuna in a non-metallic bowl, cover with 2 tablespoons of the chermoula and toss. Marinate in the fridge for 20 minutes.

Meanwhile, cook the pasta in a large saucepan of boiling salted water until al dente. Drain well and return to the pan to keep warm. Mix in the remaining chermoula and oil.

Heat a lightly oiled chargrill pan over high heat. Cook the tuna for 2 minutes on each side, or until done to your liking. Cut into 2 cm (¾ inch) cubes . and toss through the pasta with the sweet potato.

Serves 4

## Pasta with artichokes and grilled chicken

1 tablespoon olive oil
3 chicken breast fillets
500 g (1 lb 2 oz) pasta, such as
   tagliatelle or any long, flat pasta
8 slices prosciutto
280 g (10 oz) artichokes in oil, drained
   and quartered, oil reserved
150 g (5½ oz) semi-dried (sun-
   blushed) tomatoes, thinly sliced
90 g (3¼ oz) baby rocket (arugula)
2–3 tablespoons balsamic vinegar

Lightly brush a chargrill pan (griddle) or frying pan with oil and heat over high heat. Cook the chicken fillets for 6–8 minutes each side, or until they are cooked through. Thinly slice and set aside.

Cook the pasta in a large saucepan of boiling salted water until al dente. Drain the pasta and return to the pan to keep warm. Meanwhile, place the prosciutto under a hot grill (broiler) and grill (broil) for 2 minutes each side, or until crisp. Cool slightly and break into pieces.

Combine the pasta with the chicken, prosciutto, artichokes, tomato and rocket in a bowl and toss. Whisk together 3 tablespoons of the reserved artichoke oil and the balsamic vinegar and toss through the pasta mixture. Season and serve.

Serves 6

## Pappardelle with rabbit and capsicum

3 tablespoons olive oil
1 x 1 kg (2 lb 4 oz) rabbit, jointed
2 slices bacon, chopped
1 onion, sliced
2 celery stalks, chopped
1 garlic clove, crushed
2 tablespoons plain (all-purpose) flour
1 teaspoon dried marjoram
425 g (15 oz) tinned chopped
   tomatoes
125 ml (4 fl oz/½ cup) dry red wine
3 tablespoons tomato paste
   (concentrated purée)
1 red capsicum (pepper), seeded
   and sliced
1 eggplant (aubergine), quartered
   and sliced
500 g (1 lb 2 oz) pappardelle

Heat the oil in a large frying pan. Add the rabbit and brown well on all sides. Transfer to a plate. Add the bacon, onion, celery and garlic to the same pan and stir over low heat until the onion is soft.

Stir in the flour and marjoram and cook for 1 minute. Add the tomato, wine, tomato paste, 125 ml (4 fl oz/ ½ cup) water and season. Stir well.

Bring to the boil, stirring constantly. Reduce the heat and return the rabbit to the pan. Simmer, covered, for 1½ hours or until the rabbit is very tender, adding more water as required. Remove the rabbit from the sauce and allow to cool slightly. Remove the meat from the bones.

Return the rabbit meat to the sauce with the capsicum and eggplant. Simmer for another 15–20 minutes. Meanwhile, cook the pasta in a large saucepan of rapidly boiling salted water until al dente. Drain well and return to the pan to keep warm. Serve the hot sauce over the pasta.

Serves 4

# Free-form ricotta and mushroom lasagne

250 g (9 oz/1 cup) ricotta cheese
65 g (2oz/²/₃ cup) grated parmesan
  cheese
3½ tablespoons olive oil
1 onion, thinly sliced
2 garlic cloves, crushed
500 g (1 lb 2 oz) Swiss brown
  mushrooms, sliced
300 ml (10½ fl oz) Italian tomato
  pasta sauce
6 fresh lasagne sheets, cut in half,
  then cut into 12 cm (4½ inch)
  squares
200 g (7 oz) baby spinach leaves

Mix the ricotta with half the parmesan and season well. Heat 2 tablespoons oil in a large frying pan, add the onion and cook for 2 minutes, or until it softens. Add the garlic and mushrooms and cook for 1–2 minutes, or until the mushrooms start to soften. Add the pasta sauce and cook for another 5–6 minutes, or until the sauce starts to thicken. Season well.

Meanwhile, bring a deep saucepan of water to a boil, add 1 tablespoon oil and a pinch of salt. Cook the lasagne squares and cook for 2–3 minutes, or until cooked. Drain, keeping each square separate. Put the spinach in a pan with just the water clinging to the leaves. Cover and cook over medium heat for 1–2 minutes, or until the spinach has wilted.

To assemble, place a pasta square on each serving plate, then divide the mushroom sauce among the squares. Place another pasta square on top, then spread the ricotta mixture evenly over the surface, leaving a 2 cm (¾ inch) border. Divide the spinach evenly among the four servings. Finally, place another pasta square on top, brush or drizzle with the remaining oil, then sprinkle with the remaining parmesan. Season. Serve with a green salad and crusty bread.

Serves 4

# Baked seafood pasta

250 g (9 oz) fresh lasagne sheets
500 g (1 lb 2 oz) boneless fish fillets
125 g (4½ oz) scallops
500 g (1 lb 2 oz) raw prawns (shrimp),
  peeled and deveined
125 g (4½ oz) butter
1 leek, sliced
90 g (3¼ oz/¾ cup) plain (all-purpose)
  flour
500 ml (17 fl oz/2 cups) milk
500 ml (17 fl oz/2 cups) dry white wine
125 g (4½ oz/1 cup) grated cheddar
  cheese
125 ml (4 fl oz/½ cup) pouring
  (whipping) cream
60 g (2¼ oz) grated parmesan cheese
2 tablespoons chopped flat-leaf
  (Italian) parsley

Preheat the oven to 180°C (350°F/ Gas 4). Grease a shallow 24 cm x 30 cm (9½ inch x 12 inch) ovenproof dish and line with lasagne sheets, breaking them to fill any gaps. Chop the fish and scallops into bite-sized pieces. Chop the prawns.

Melt the butter in a large saucepan and cook the leek, stirring, for 1 minute. Add the flour and cook, stirring, for 1 minute. Remove from the heat and slowly stir in the milk and wine until smooth. Return to medium heat and stir constantly until the sauce boils and thickens. Reduce the heat and simmer for 3 minutes. Stir in the cheddar cheese and seafood, season and simmer for 1 minute.

Spoon half the seafood sauce over the lasagne sheets. Top with another layer of lasagne sheets. Continue layering the sauce and the sheets, finishing with lasagne sheets.

Pour the cream over the top. Sprinkle with the combined parmesan and parsley and bake for 30 minutes, or until bubbling and golden.

Serves 4–6

## Creamy chicken and peppercorn pappardelle

2 chicken breast fillets (420 g in total)
30 g (1 oz) butter
1 onion, halved and thinly sliced
2 tablespoons drained green
  peppercorns, slightly crushed
125 ml (4 fl oz/½ cup) white wine
300 ml (10½ fl oz) pouring
  (whipping) cream
400 g (14 oz) fresh pappardelle
80 g (2¾ oz/⅓ cup) sour cream
  (optional)
2 tablespoons chopped chives

Cut the chicken in half so that you have four flat fillets and season. Melt the butter in a frying pan, add the chicken and cook for 3 minutes each side, or until lightly browned and cooked through. Remove from the pan, cut into slices and keep warm.

Add the onion and peppercorns to the same pan and cook over medium heat for 3 minutes, or until the onion has softened slightly. Add the wine and cook for 1 minute, or until reduced by half. Stir in the cream and cook for 4–5 minutes, or until thickened slightly, then season with salt and black pepper. Meanwhile, cook the pasta in a large saucepan of boiling water until al dente, then drain. Mix together the pasta, chicken and any juices and cream sauce. Divide the pasta among serving bowls, top with a dollop of sour cream and sprinkle with chives.

Serves 4

# Blue cheese and walnut lasagnette

375 g (13 oz) lasagnette
100 g (3½ oz/1 cup) walnuts
40 g (1½ oz) butter
3 French shallots (eschalots),
  finely chopped
1 tablespoon brandy or cognac
250 ml (9 fl oz/1 cup) crème fraîche
200 g (7 oz) Gorgonzola cheese,
  crumbled
70 g (2½ oz) baby spinach leaves

Preheat the oven to 200°C (400°F/ Gas 6). Cook the pasta in a large saucepan of boiling salted water until al dente. Drain, return to the pan and keep warm.

Meanwhile, place the walnuts on a baking tray and roast for 5 minutes, or until golden and toasted. Cool, then roughly chop.

Heat the butter in a large saucepan, add the shallots and cook over medium heat for 1–2 minutes, or until soft, taking care not to brown. Add the brandy and simmer for 1 minute, then stir in the crème fraîche and Gorgonzola. Cook for 3–4 minutes, or until the cheese has melted and the sauce has thickened.

Stir in the spinach and toasted walnuts, reserving 1 tablespoon for garnish. Heat gently until the spinach has just wilted. Season and gently mix the sauce through the pasta. Divide among serving plates and sprinkle with the reserved walnuts.

Serves 4

## Pappardelle with salmon and gremolata

1 handful flat-leaf (Italian) parsley
  leaves, chopped
3 teaspoons finely grated lemon zest
2 garlic cloves, finely chopped
400 g (14 oz) pappardelle
3½ tablespoons extra virgin olive oil
500 g (1 lb 2 oz) salmon fillet

To make the gremolata, put the parsley, lemon zest and garlic in a bowl and mix together well.

Cook the pasta in a large saucepan of rapidly boiling salted water until al dente. Drain well and return to the pan. Add 3 tablespoons of the olive oil and toss gently. Add the gremolata to the pan with the pasta and toss.

Remove the skin and any bones from the salmon. Heat the remaining olive oil in a frying pan over medium heat. Cook the salmon for 3–4 minutes, turning once during cooking. Take care not to overcook the fish. Flake the salmon into large pieces and toss through the pasta. Season.

Serves 4

## Free-form wild mushroom lasagne

10 g (¼ oz) dried porcini mushrooms
350 g (12 oz) mixed wild mushrooms
   (such as shiitake, oyster
   and Swiss brown)
30 g (1 oz) butter
1 small onion, halved and thinly sliced
1 tablespoon chopped thyme
3 egg yolks
125 ml (4 fl oz/½ cup) thick
   (double/heavy) cream
100 g (3½ oz/1 cup) grated
   parmesan cheese
8 fresh lasagne sheets
   (each sheet 10 cm x 25 cm/
   4 inches x 10 inches)

Soak the porcini in 3 tablespoons boiling water for 15 minutes. Strain through a sieve, reserving the liquid. Cut the larger mushrooms in half.

Heat the butter in a frying pan over medium heat. Cook the onion for 2 minutes, or until just soft. Add the thyme, mushrooms and porcini and cook for about 1–2 minutes, or until softened. Add the reserved mushroom liquid and cook for 2 minutes, or until the liquid has evaporated. Set aside.

Beat the egg yolks, cream and half the parmesan in a large bowl. Cook the pasta in a large saucepan of boiling salted water until al dente. Drain well and toss gently in the egg mixture. Reheat the mushrooms.

To serve, place one sheet of folded lasagne on a plate. Top with some mushrooms, then another sheet of folded lasagne. Drizzle with any remaining egg mixture and sprinkle with the remaining parmesan.

Serves 4

## Roast duck with fresh pappardelle

250 g (9 oz) baby bok choy (pak choy), washed and leaves separated
600 g (1 lb 5 oz) fresh pappardelle
1 Chinese roast duck, skin removed (see Note)
80 ml (2½ fl oz/⅓ cup) peanut oil
3 garlic cloves, crushed
3 teaspoons finely chopped ginger
1 handful coriander (cilantro) leaves, chopped
2 tablespoons hoisin sauce
2 tablespoons oyster sauce

Bring a large saucepan of water to the boil and blanch the bok choy for 1–2 minutes, or until tender, but still crisp. Remove with a slotted spoon and keep warm.

Meanwhile, cook the pasta in a large saucepan of boiling salted water until al dente. Drain well and return to the pan to keep warm.

Remove the duck meat from the bones and finely shred. Heat the peanut oil in a small saucepan over high heat and bring it up to smoking point. Remove from the heat and allow to cool for 1 minute, then swirl in the garlic and ginger to infuse the oil. Be careful not to allow the garlic to burn or it will turn bitter.

Pour the hot oil over the pasta and add the bok choy, duck, coriander, hoisin and oyster sauces. Toss well, season and serve immediately.

Serves 4–6

Note: Chinese roast duck can be bought from Asian speciality shops.

## Smoked salmon stracci in Champagne sauce

375 g (13 oz) fresh stracci (see Notes)
1 tablespoon olive oil
2 large garlic cloves, crushed
125 ml (4 fl oz/½ cup) Champagne
250 ml (9 fl oz/1 cup) thick
  (double/heavy) cream
200 g (7 oz) smoked salmon,
  cut into thin strips
2 tablespoons baby capers in brine,
  drained, rinsed and patted dry
2 tablespoons chopped chives
2 tablespoons chopped dill

Cook the pasta in a large saucepan of rapidly boiling salted water until al dente. Drain well and return to the pan to keep warm.

Meanwhile, heat the oil in a large frying pan and cook the garlic over medium heat for 30 seconds. Pour in the Champagne and cook for 2–3 minutes, or until the liquid is reduced slightly. Add the cream and cook for 3–4 minutes, or until the sauce has thickened.

Add the sauce, salmon, capers and herbs to the hot pasta and toss gently. Season.

Serves 4

Notes: Stracci is sold fresh and dried—either is suitable for this recipe—or you can use fresh or dried fettuccine or tagliatelle. Dried lasagne sheets can also be used instead of stracci. Break them into ragged pieces measuring about 8 cm x 13 cm (3 inches x 5 inches).

## Pasta with lamb shank, rosemary and red wine ragù

1½ tablespoons olive oil
1 large onion, finely chopped
1 large carrot, finely diced
2 celery stalks, finely diced
2 bay leaves
1.5 kg (3 lb 5 oz) lamb shanks,
  trimmed of excess fat
4 garlic cloves, finely chopped
1 tablespoon finely chopped rosemary
750 ml (26 fl oz/3 cups) dry red wine
1 litre (35 fl oz/4 cups) beef stock
500 ml (17 fl oz/2 cups) Italian
  tomato pasta sauce
½ teaspoon finely grated lemon zest
500 g (1 lb 2 oz) pappardelle or any
  ribbon-shaped pasta
flat-leaf (Italian) parsley leaves,
  for garnishing

Heat 1 tablespoon of the oil in a large, deep saucepan. Add the onion, carrot, celery and bay leaves and cook over medium heat, stirring often, for about 10 minutes, or until the onion is lightly browned. Remove from the pan. Heat a little more oil in the pan and cook the shanks in two batches, turning occasionally, for 15 minutes, or until browned. Remove from the pan.

Add the garlic and rosemary to the pan and cook for 30 seconds, or until lightly golden and fragrant. Return the vegetables to the pan, then stir in the wine, stock, tomato sauce, zest and 250 ml (9 fl oz/1 cup) of water. Using a wooden spoon, scrape up any sediment stuck to the base of the pan. Add the shanks and bring to the boil—removing any scum that rises to the surface. Reduce the heat and simmer, uncovered, for 2¼ hours, or until the lamb is very tender and the sauce is thick and glossy.

Meanwhile, cook the pasta in a saucepan of boiling salted water until al dente. Drain well and keep warm.

Remove the shanks from the sauce and remove the meat from the bones. Return the meat to the sauce and heat through. Season. Toss the pasta through the sauce. Serve with parsley.

Serves 6–8

# Free-form pumpkin, spinach and ricotta lasagne

3 tablespoons olive oil
1.5 kg (3 lb 5 oz) butternut pumpkin
  (winter squash), cut into 1.5 cm
  (⁵/₈ inch) dice
500 g (1 lb 2 oz) English spinach
  leaves, thoroughly washed
4 fresh lasagne sheets
  (each sheet 12cm x 20 cm/
  5 inches x 8 inches)
500 g (1 lb 2 oz/2 cups) ricotta cheese
2 tablespoons pouring
  (whipping) ream
3 tablespoons grated parmesan
  cheese
pinch ground nutmeg

Heat the oil in a non-stick frying pan over medium heat. Add the pumpkin and toss. Cook, stirring occasionally, for 15 minutes, or until tender (don't worry if the pumpkin is slightly mashed). Season and keep warm.

Cook the spinach in a large saucepan of boiling water for 30 seconds, or until wilted. Using a slotted spoon, transfer to a bowl of cold water. Drain well and squeeze out as much excess water as possible. Finely chop the spinach. Add the lasagne sheets to the pan of boiling water and cook, stirring occasionally, until al dente. Drain and lay the sheets side-by-side on a clean tea towel. Cut each sheet widthways into thirds.

Put the ricotta, cream, parmesan, spinach and nutmeg in a small pan. Stir over low heat for 2–3 minutes, or until warmed through. Work quickly to assemble. Place a piece of lasagne on the base of each plate. Using half the pumpkin, top each of the sheets, then cover with another piece of lasagne. Use half the ricotta mixture to spread over the lasagne sheets, then add another lasagne piece.

Top with the remaining pumpkin, then remaining ricotta mixture. Season well and serve immediately.

Serves 4

## Pappardelle with salami, leek and provolone cheese

375 g (13 oz) pappardelle
2 tablespoons olive oil
2 leeks, thinly sliced (including some
of the green section)
2 tablespoons white wine
800 g (1 lb 12 oz) tinned diced
tomatoes
150 g (5½ oz) sliced mild salami,
cut into strips
1 large handful basil leaves, torn
125 g (4½ oz) provolone cheese,
cut into 3 cm (1¼ inch) wide strips
30 g (1 oz) grated parmesan cheese

Cook the pasta in a large saucepan
of rapidly boiling salted water until
al dente. Drain well and return to the
pan to keep warm.

Meanwhile, heat the oil in a large deep
frying pan over low heat. Add the leek
and cook for 4 minutes, or until soft
but not browned. Increase the heat
to medium, add the wine and stir until
almost evaporated.

Add the tomato and salami. Season
and simmer for 5 minutes, or until
reduced slightly. Toss the tomato
sauce mixture, basil and provolone
lightly through the pasta. Sprinkle
with the parmesan.

Serves 4

# Seafood lasagne

1 tablespoon olive oil
2 garlic cloves, crushed
1/4 teaspoon saffron threads
600 ml (21 oz) Italian tomato
    pasta sauce
750 g (1 lb 10 oz) mixed raw seafood,
    cut into bite-sized pieces (use
    scallops and peeled prawns or
    prepared marinara mix)
4 fresh lasagne sheets, cut into twelve
    10 cm x 16 cm (4 inch x 6¼ inch)
    rectangles
120 g (4¼ oz) English spinach leaves
185 g (6½ oz) mascarpone cheese
90 g (3¼ oz) grated parmesan cheese

Heat the oil in a large saucepan, add
the garlic, saffron and pasta sauce,
reduce the heat and simmer for
8 minutes, or until thickened slightly.
Add the seafood and cook for
2 minutes, or until cooked, then
season. Remove from the heat.

Cook the pasta in a large saucepan of
boiling salted water for 1–2 minutes,
or until al dente. Remove and arrange
the sheets on a tray to prevent them
sticking. Blanch the spinach in the
same saucepan of boiling water for
30 seconds. Remove with tongs,
transfer to a colander and drain well.

To assemble, lay a pasta rectangle on
each of four ovenproof serving plates.
Spread half the mascarpone over the
pasta sheets. Top with half the
spinach and half the seafood sauce.
Sprinkle with one-third of the
parmesan. Repeat to give two layers,
finishing with a third pasta sheet.
Sprinkle with the remaining cheese.
Place under a medium grill (broiler)
for 2 minutes, or until the cheese is
slightly melted. Serve immediately.

Serves 4

## Pappardelle with lobster and saffron cream sauce

400 g (14 oz) pappardelle
60 g (2¼ oz) butter
4 large garlic cloves, crushed
250 g (9 oz) Swiss brown mushrooms, sliced
500 g (1 lb 2 oz) fresh or frozen lobster tail meat or raw bug tails, cut into chunks
125 ml (4 fl oz/½ cup) dry white wine
½ teaspoon saffron threads
700 ml (24 fl oz) thickened (whipping) cream
2 egg yolks

Cook the pasta in a large saucepan of rapidly boiling salted water until al dente. Drain well and return to the pan to keep warm.

Meanwhile, melt the butter in a large deep frying pan, add the garlic and mushrooms and cook over medium heat for 2–3 minutes, or until soft. Add the lobster and cook for 4–5 minutes, or until just cooked through. Remove from the pan.

Add the wine and saffron to the pan, scraping the bottom to collect any bits. Bring to the boil and cook for 2–3 minutes, or until reduced. Add the cream, reduce the heat and simmer for 5 minutes. Whisk through the egg yolks until thickened. Return the lobster mixture to the pan and stir until warmed through. Drain the pasta and divide among serving dishes. Spoon on the lobster sauce and season to taste. Serve immediately.

Serves 4–6

# Index

# INDEX

Published in 2011 by Murdoch Books Pty Limited

Murdoch Books Australia
Pier 8/9, 23 Hickson Road
Millers Point NSW 2000
Phone: +61 (0)2 8220 2000
Fax: +61 (0)2 8220 2558
www.murdochbooks.com.au

Murdoch Books UK Limited
Erico House, 6th Floor
93-99 Upper Richmond Road
Putney, London SW15 2TG
Phone: +44 (0)20 8785 5995
Fax: +44 (0)20 8785 5985
www.murdochbooks.co.uk

Publisher: Lynn Lewis
Designer: Transformer
Photography (cover): Stuart Scott
Stylist (cover): Louise Bickle
Production: Shannon Haworth

National Library of Australia Cataloguing-in-Publication entry
Title: Chunky pasta.
ISBN: 9781742663616 (hbk.)
Notes: Includes index.
Subjects: Cooking (Pasta)
Dewey Number: 641.822

Printed by Main Choice Hop Kee Factory Co. Ltd.
PRINTED IN CHINA

Cover credits: All fabrics from No Chintz, Sydney.

IMPORTANT: Those who might be at risk from the effects of salmonella poisoning (the elderly,
pregnant women, young children and those suffering from immune deficiency diseases)
should consult their doctor with any concerns about eating raw eggs.

OVEN GUIDE: You may find cooking times vary depending on the oven you are using. For fan-forced
ovens, as a general rule, set the oven temperature to 20°C (35°F) lower than indicated in the recipe.